(preceeding page)
Dizzy and Paul Dean

Never shy about posing for photographers, Dizzy Dean takes matters into his own hands before an afternoon game at Wrigley Field.

CARDINALS Collection

100 Years of St. Louis Cardinals Images

by

Mark Stang

ORANGE FRAZER PRESS
Wilmington, Ohio

ISBN: 1-882203-85-2

Copyright © 2002 by Mark M. Stang

Orange Frazer Press, Inc.
Box 214
37½ West Main Street
Wilmington, Ohio 45177

Telephone 1.800.852.9332 for price and shipping information
Web Site: www.orangefrazer.com
E-mail address: editor@orangefrazer.com

Library of Congress Cataloging-in-Publication Data

Stang, Mark (Mark Michael)
Cardinals collection : 100 years of St. Louis Cardinal images / by Mark Stang.
p. cm
Includes index
ISBN 1-882203-85-2
1.St. Louis Cardinals (Baseball team)--Biography--Portraits. 2. St. Louis Cardinals
(Baseball team)--History--20th century--Pictorial works. I. Title: 100 years of St. Louis
Cardinal images.

GV875.S3 S75 2002
796.357'64'0977866--dc21   2002029253

Printed in Canada

For all the anonymous photographers whose work graces these pages,
With thanks and admiration.

-MS

Introduction

In the faces on these pages lie the stories, the legends and the lore of St. Louis Cardinals baseball in the 20th Century. Some of the photographs have brief tales to tell; other pictures, as the old saying suggests, are worth a thousand words.

A few of the images are familiar, but I have included dozens of previously unpublished photos and many others that were published only once, long ago. The 225 images in this book, culled from 15 public and private collections, are what I believe to be the best available photographs of St. Louis players through the century.

It is important to note what this book is not. It is not meant to be the 200 greatest players in St. Louis Cardinals history. It is not meant to be the greatest moments in the Cardinals history, nor a history of baseball in St. Louis. There are, and will be, other books covering these particular topics.

This book is a collection of photos that include the famous, the not so famous and the long forgotten personalities in Cardinals history. I chose photos for a variety of reasons. Some players were obvious choices. A book of St. Louis Cardinals images couldn't very well omit stars like Stan Musial, Ducky Medwick, Johnny Mize or Mark McGwire. But

beyond the Hall of Fame caliber players, there are dozens of forgotten personalities whose stories are just as compelling.

When I discovered the stories of players like Austin McHenry, or accomplishments like those of Bill Doak, I knew they had to be included. People behind the scenes, the owners and managers, also offered fascinating stories. Woven together, I sought to paint a picture that did justice to the rich tapestry that has been the tradition of Cardinals baseball.

I came to see myself as a baseball archeologist, uncovering photographic treasures hidden for decades in dusty old files. The opportunity to bring a long forgotten photo back to life made my search for the finest available images a rewarding one. I hope you will agree.

So I now present to you the obvious and the obscure, the famous and the forgotten personalities that have shaped the past century of this city's rich baseball heritage.

Mark Stang
2002

Acknowledgments

This project would not have been possible without the assistance of many individuals. I was given complete access to the photo and clip files at *The Sporting News* in St. Louis, where archivist Steve Gietshier and Jim Meier offered invaluable help. Many thanks to Tim Wiles and Pat Kelly (and their staffs) at the National Baseball Library in Cooperstown for their assistance.

I am deeply indebted to several professional photographers whose work appears in these pages. Doug McWilliams, Bill Knight and Skip Trombetti all provided key images.

Vintage photo collectors Dan Knoll, Dennis Goldstein, Mike Mumby, and Bill Loughman graciously shared their troves of treasured images with me and Cardinals fans everywhere. Mark Rucker at Transcendental Graphics provided his usual superior service and the SABR-Ottoson photo collection filled in some of the gaps.

My thanks to Charles Brown at the University of Missouri-St. Louis' Mercantile Library for his assistance with the defunct *Globe Democrat* photo files. In addition, Ellen Soeteber, Arnie Robbins and Larry Coyne generously allowed me access to the photo files at *The St. Louis Post-Dispatch*. Former librarian Ray Zwick at *The Cincinnati Enquirer* helped, as well.

A deep debt of gratitude is again owed to Rosemary Goudreau for her tireless editing of the text. My thanks also to Phil Wood for his thorough fact-checking. Thanks also to Elaine Olund at Lamson Design for the original cover concept. Thanks to Monte Pietrosky and his staff at Litho-Craft in Cincinnati for their assistance with the photo imaging.

The format used in *Cardinals Collection* owes its inspiration to a 1999 publication I co-authored with Greg Rhodes entitled: *Reds in Black and White, 100 Years of Cincinnati Reds Images.* That book, in turn, owes a debt of gratitude to the classic work by Neal and Constance McCabe, *Baseball's Golden Age: The Photographs of Charles M. Conlon* (published in 1993).

Finally, the behind-the-scenes star, as always, is Ryan Asher. His technical wizardry and tireless dedication to providing the best possible image is evident on every page. Ryan also executed the page layout and the cover design.

To all these folks, I offer my sincere appreciation for their hard work and cooperation in making this project possible.

Patsy Donovan
Outfielder, 1900 - 03
Manager, 1901 - 03

The winning tradition of the St. Louis Cardinals got off to a rocky start.

At the start of the last century, the Cardinals were among the worst teams in the National League. Between 1900 and 1920, the team had only four winning seasons and never placed higher than third.

Trouble began soon after Cardinals owner Frank Robison moved his team from Cleveland in 1899. Two years later, a rival league started up and began luring away players with higher salaries. Most of the Cardinals' best players switched to the American League. Most, but not veteran Patsy Donovan, who'd established himself as one of the league's best hitters, fielders and base runners.

Donovan played in Pittsburgh before joining the Cardinals. In his seven seasons there, Donovan hit over .300 six times and stole 272 bases. He was the Pirates' manager in 1899, but when the club was sold, the new owners traded him to St. Louis.

His first year as a Cardinal, Donovan batted .316 and led the league with 45 stolen bases. Still, the depleted team finished fifth. The next year, Donovan was named player-manager and he led the team to a fourth-place finish. By 1903, however, the club's poor finances and weak lineup left the Cardinals at the bottom of the standings and Donovan was replaced.

Donovan spent the next four years managing Washington, then Brooklyn, before becoming manager of the Boston Red Sox in 1910. He lasted only two seasons in Boston, though, because once again, a change in ownership led to a change in direction. Considered an excellent judge of young talent, Donovan became a scout. His lasting contribution was acquiring the players who delivered American League pennants to Boston in three of the next five seasons.

In 1914, Donovan spotted a 19-year-old pitcher named George Herman Ruth toiling in the minors at Baltimore. In town to scout someone else, Donovan was so impressed by the young Ruth's skills that he immediately wired the club's owners and urged them to make a quick deal for him. Boston purchased Babe Ruth and two other players for $20,000.

Charles "Kid" Nichols
Pitcher-Manager, 1904 - 05

Before joining the Cardinals, Charles Nichols pitched in Boston where he won 328 games in 12 years. Over one seven-year stretch, he won 30 or more games every year, a streak unequaled to this day.

Nichols' reputation for wins and endurance began almost immediately after he joined the Boston Beaneaters, later re-named the "Braves," at the age of 20. As a rookie in 1890, Nichols won 27 games and led the league with seven shut-outs. He pitched more than 400 innings in each of his first five seasons and developed a reputation for finishing what he started.

In 1892, he threw 50 complete games in 51 starts, including three complete games on three straight days in three different cities. And in 1900, at the age of 30, Nichols became the youngest pitcher ever to achieve 300 career wins, a record that will almost certainly never be equaled.

Nichols helped Boston win five pennants during his 12 seasons there.

But in 1902, Nichols left Boston to assume partial ownership of the minor-league team in his native Kansas City. There, he served as player-manager for two seasons before financial troubles caused the team to fold. Nichols then agreed to join the Cardinals as a pitcher and the manager of the 1904 team.

His first year in St. Louis, the 34-year-old Nichols won 21 games on the mound and led the team to a fifth-place finish. But the next year, the Cardinals got off to a poor start. By June, the team had a 19-29 record. On the road in Cincinnati, Nichols was assigned to watch the ticket gate, a custom of the day for pitchers on their off days. (Visiting clubs wanted to be sure that the home team didn't adjust attendance figures and short their share of gate receipts.) Nichols decided his time was better spent at the racetrack. When he returned to the ballpark, he was fired on the spot.

Nichols caught on with the Phillies, where he won another 10 games before retiring after the 1906 season, having amassed 360 career victories. He returned to Kansas City and ran a string of bowling alleys. Nichols was elected to the Hall of Fame in 1949.

Ed Konetchy
First baseman, 1907 - 1913

Ed Konetchy was a powerful slugger whose physique earned him the nickname "Big Ed."

Signed by the Cardinals after only two seasons in the minor leagues, Konetchy took over first base midway through the 1907 season and quickly became the team's most reliable hitter. In 1910, he had a 20-game hitting streak and batted .302. The next year, he led the National League with 38 doubles. Installed as the team's clean-up hitter, Konetchy's slashing line drives soon became his trademark. He also showed unusual speed for a man his size, stealing at least 25 bases four times. But he was surrounded by mediocre talent. The Cardinals managed only one winning season during his seven years in St. Louis.

Following the 1913 season, Konetchy was traded to Pittsburgh. After a single season with the Pirates, he jumped to the upstart Federal League for one year before rejoining the National League in 1916 with the Boston Braves. In 1919, Konetchy was sold to Brooklyn, where he soon put together a string of 10 consecutive hits. He retired from the majors after the 1921 season and spent the next six years playing in the minor leagues. In 1925, at the age of 39, he led Fort Worth to the Texas League championship by hitting 41 home runs and driving in 166 runs.

Roger Bresnahan
Catcher-Manager, 1909 - 1912

Roger Bresnahan is best known for two things: serving as Christy Mathewson's catcher during the New York Giants' glory days and introducing shin guards as a regular piece of equipment behind the plate.

Bresnahan, an aggressive catcher with a fiery personality, was the type of player the Cardinals thought they needed after finishing last in 1907 and 1908. Bresnahan came to St. Louis in 1909 as player-manager and his temperament became quickly familiar. Frustrated by his team's poor play, Bresnahan fought constantly with umpires and was frequently suspended by the league's president. The emotion had little effect, though, as the Cardinals won just 54 games and finished in seventh place.

Using what he'd learned behind the plate, Bresnahan focused on developing the Cardinals' young pitching staff, a move that paid off. By the middle of 1911, the club found itself three games out of first and attendance soared. Although the team eventually finished fifth, it had its first winning season in more than a decade. Club owners rewarded Bresnahan with a five-year contract that paid $10,000 a year along with 10 percent of the team's profits. But the next year, beset by injuries and player hold-outs, the Cardinals reverted to form and fell to the bottom of the standings. At season's end, Bresnahan was fired. He demanded to be paid for the remaining four years of his contract, but eventually settled for $20,000.

Bresnahan signed with the Chicago Cubs, where he managed for a single season in 1915. Later, he returned to his native Toledo and bought controlling interest in the minor league team, which he ran for eight years before returning to the majors as a coach with the Giants and the Tigers. He died in 1944 at the age of 65. He was elected to the Hall of Fame the next year.

Bob Harmon
Pitcher, 1909 - 1913

Bob Harmon's big-league education began after he threw a no-hitter for the minor-league Shreveport Pirates in 1909.

The Cardinals immediately brought him to St. Louis and although he was used sparingly his first season, the 21-year-old rookie got to see the country. Years later, Harmon recalled his first visit to New York City. "I had pitched against the Giants in New York and won. That night, figuring I might never get back to the big city, I went with a group of the boys to Coney Island to see the sights. While there, we came across a fellow in a cage who was dodging balls. If you hit him, down he went into the water. Sure, I threw and threw until I got a sore arm. But a few days later, I went to Atlantic City, swam all day, got a

terrific sunburn, but burned the soreness out of my arm."

The next year, the young right-hander won 13 games, but led the National League in walks. In 1911, however, Harmon became the ace of the Cardinals pitching staff, winning 23 games. It was the most wins in one season by a Cardinals pitcher since 1899. In 1912, he again led the pitching staff with 18 wins. All this for a team that won just 64 games and finished sixth. It was also Harmon's last big season in the major leagues. In 1913, he went 8-21 and was traded to Pittsburgh at season's end. Harmon had four straight losing years with the Pirates and retired in 1918. He returned to Louisiana and invested in oil. By the early 1920s, Harmon had become one of the state's leading dairy farmers.

Miller Huggins
Second baseman, 1910 - 1916
Manager, 1913 - 1916

Miller Huggins never let his small size get in the way of great things on the ballfield.

His drive showed through as a teenager in Ohio when on Sundays, he played baseball under an assumed name to avoid the wrath of his father, a devout Methodist. Later, after earning a law degree from the University of Cincinnati, he instead chose to play ball in the minor leagues. And after hitting over .300 for three straight years for St. Paul, he joined the Cincinnati Reds in 1904.

As the Reds' everyday second baseman, Huggins used his quickness to cover a lot of ground, earning him the nickname "Little Mr. Everywhere." At the plate, he developed a keen batting eye as the Reds' lead-off hitter. Twice, he led the National League in walks.

In St. Louis, manager Roger Bresnahan put together a five-player trade that brought Huggins to the Cardinals in 1910. Soon, his hustle and affinity for getting on base made him a favorite of the fans as well as the team's owners. When Bresnahan was fired after the 1912 season, Huggins was tapped to take his place. In 1914, he led the Cardinals to a third-place finish, their highest ranking in almost four decades. That year, Huggins again led the league in walks and stole 32 bases, but it was his last season as an everyday player.

Huggins' future with the team came to an end in 1917 after the Cardinals placed third and the owners decided to sell the club. Nevertheless, Huggins' fortunes continued to rise. The owners of the New York Yankees, a franchise that struggled to avoid the cellar every season, had noted his success with the Cardinals and offered him a contract that doubled his salary. Over the next 12 seasons, Huggins' talent for evaluating ballplayers — combined with the Yankees' deep pockets — produced six American League pennants and three World Series titles.

In 1929, Huggins suddenly grew severely ill. A cut below his eye brought on blood poisoning and, on September 25, Miller Huggins died at the age of 50. So great was his legacy that his was the first monument erected in centerfield at Yankee Stadium. He was elected to the Hall of Fame in 1964.

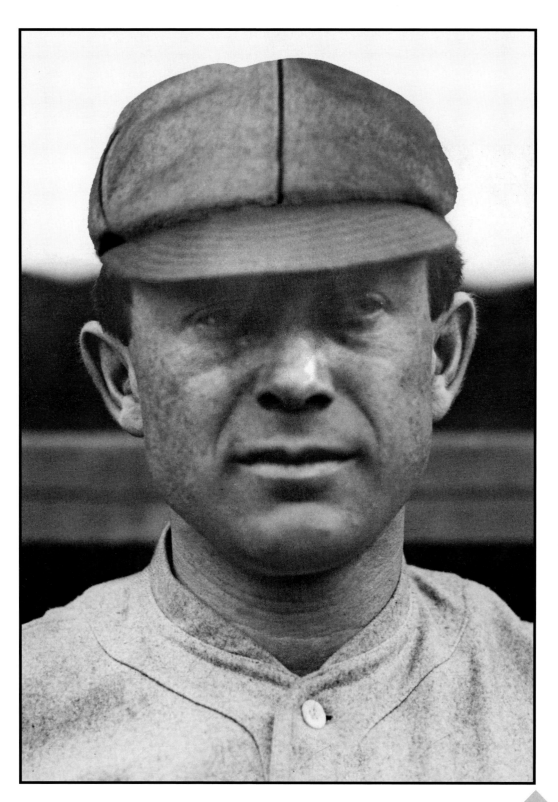

Harry "Slim" Sallee
Pitcher, 1908 - 1916

"Slim" Sallee was a tall string-bean whose pinpoint control kept him in the major leagues for 14 seasons. The Cardinals signed him after he won 22 games for Williamsport in 1907. His slender build and long arms gave his left-handed delivery a deceptive motion dubbed a "crossfire pitch." During his first several seasons in the majors, Sallee's constant drinking kept him from winning more games.

But by 1911, his third full season in the majors, Sallee had settled down and become a regular winner for the Cardinals. Over the next five years he won a total of 80 games for St. Louis, a team that regularly finished near the bottom of the standings. But the strict discipline imposed by manager Miller Huggins rubbed a free spirit like Sallee the wrong way. Early in 1916, during a road trip in New York, Sallee disappeared from the team and was suspended by Huggins. Threatening to retire from the game rather than continue playing for Huggins, Sallee was eventually sold to the New York Giants for $12,000.

There he won 18 games for the Giants in 1917. Two years later, Sallee was once again traded, this time to the Cincinnati Reds. He had the best year of his career, winning 21 games, as the Reds won the National League pennant. In the 1919 World Series against the infamous Chicago "Black Sox," Sallee won Game 2, but lost Game 7. He finished his career in the majors with the Giants and retired after a single season back in the minor leagues in 1922.

He returned to his home outside Cincinnati and ran a tavern for many years until his death in 1950.

Mrs. Helene Robison Britton
Owner, 1911 - 1916

When Cardinals owner Frank Robison passed away in 1908, his brother Stanley assumed ownership of the team. When Stanley died just three years later, his niece, Helene, assumed control of the club, becoming the first female owner of a major league baseball franchise.

Mrs. Britton, dubbed "Lady Bee" by the press, was a strong and independent woman active in the suffragette movement. From her stately mansion on Lindell Avenue, she quietly began to oversee the operation of the floundering franchise. She temporarily made her husband president of the club, although she later divorced him and took over the team herself. She represented the club at the annual ownership meetings in New York, where as the only woman in a sport dominated by men, she instantly became the object of considerable attention. And when Roger Bresnahan responded to her criticism of his management style with a vulgar string of profanity, she fired him on the spot despite having to buy out the remaining four years of his contract.

But the team's uneven play and the onset of World War I kept fans away. In addition, the two-year experiment of the rival Federal League, which fielded a franchise in St. Louis, siphoned off several key players. By the fall of 1916, Mrs. Britton had had enough. She announced she was selling the team and the ballpark. Cardinals manager Miller Huggins tried to put together the financing to buy the club, but in the end, "Lady Bee" sold the team to a group of local investors for $375,000.

Lee "Specs" Meadows
Pitcher, 1915 - 1919

Lee Meadows was the first ballplayer of the 20th Century to wear glasses on the playing field. When he first took the mound in 1915, he was taunted by fans and players alike. Batters said they feared for their safety. And the prevailing sentiment was that a pitcher who needed help seeing the plate could never be a major-league success. Over the next 13 seasons, Meadows proved them wrong.

Utilizing a sidearm delivery, Meadows' best pitch was a devastating curveball that he mixed with a spitball, still legal at the time. In 1916, Meadows led the National League in appearances, but despite an ERA of 2.58, his 23 losses were also tops. It is a mark of how bad the Cardinals were that season that Meadows' 12 wins led the pitching staff.

Early in 1919, a slow start led the Cardinals to trade Meadows to the lowly Phillies. Pitching for another bad team kept his record below .500 for his three-plus seasons in Philadelphia.

Late in 1923, he was traded again, this time to Pittsburgh. Given a chance to pitch for a contender, Meadows put together the best three years of his career. In 1925, the Pirates won the NL pennant and Meadows won 19 games. The following year, he went 20-9. The Pirates returned to the World Series in 1927, spurred by another 19 victories from the big left-hander. That year, Meadows led the league in starts and complete games. But it was his last season as a regular. By 1929, arm problems landed him in the minor leagues, where he spent the next four years before retiring at the age of 37. He moved to Florida, managed briefly in the minor leagues and later worked for the Internal Revenue Service.

Frank "Pancho" Snyder
Catcher, 1912 - 1919; 1927

Texan Frank Snyder's best years behind the plate came after he left St. Louis.

Promoted to the majors at age 19, Snyder had two brief trials with the Cardinals before earning the everyday job in 1914. Powerfully built and possessing a strong throwing arm, Snyder was one of the premier defensive catchers of his era. His best year with the Cardinals came in 1915, when he batted .298, slugged 22 doubles and caught 144 of a possible 154 games. But injuries caught up with him and cost him almost all of the 1918 season. The Cardinals, desperate for pitching help, traded Snyder to the New York Giants early in the 1919 season. It proved a costly mistake.

In New York, Snyder helped anchor a Giants dynasty that went to the World Series four straight years starting in 1921. Snyder's .364 average in the 1921 World Series led the team. He batted over .300 in three seasons, including .343 in 1922.

In 1927, at the age of 33, Snyder returned to St. Louis for one final season, but played in only 63 games before retiring. He managed the minor-league Houston Buffaloes to a pennant in 1928 before returning to the Giants as a coach for nine years. During the war years, he again managed in the minors before taking a sales job with a brewery in his native San Antonio. Snyder died in 1962 at the age of 68.

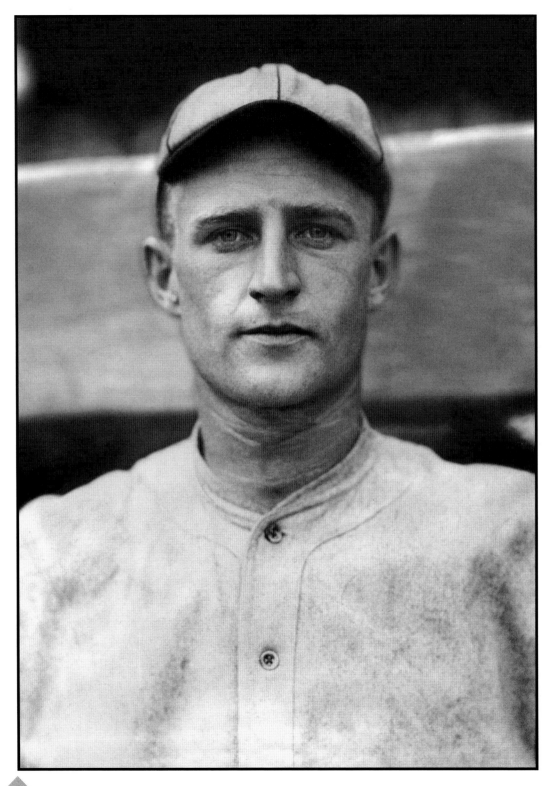

Bill Doak
Pitcher, 1913 - 1924; 1929

"Spittin' Bill" Doak became a 20-game winner for the Cardinals by mastering the spitball. But his career in St. Louis was filled with curves.

The Cardinals bought Doak's contract from Akron, where he'd been banished by the Reds after allowing two runs in his only two innings of major-league work. Desperate for pitching help, the Cardinals gave Doak a shot midway through the 1913 season. He managed to throw five complete games, including one shutout, but ended the year with a 2-8 record. No one could have predicted what Doak would do the next season.

In 1914, at age 23, Doak blossomed into one of the National League's most dominant pitchers. He threw seven shut-outs, went 19-6 and led the league with a 1.72 ERA. He defeated the Phillies' legendary pitcher Grover Cleveland Alexander and twice beat Giants ace Christy Mathewson. In a day when games were routinely played in well under two hours, Doak worked slowly and deliberately on the mound, pausing repeatedly to wipe his brow with the red handkerchief he kept in his hip pocket.

Over the next five years, Doak's record slipped to an unimpressive 66-75, a record that better reflected the Cardinals' lack of hitting. He won 20 games in 1920 and 15 the next year, but he was traded to Brooklyn after winning only 11 and eight games over the next two seasons.

Doak later moved to Florida to oversee his business interests, but when the state's land boom of the mid-1920s went bust, he returned to Brooklyn for the 1927 season and won 11 games. Two years later, after a brief return to St. Louis, he hung up his glove for good. Doak retired to Florida and operated a confectionary store in Bradenton for many years.

Rogers Hornsby
1917

More than six decades after he last played the game, Rogers Hornsby is universally regarded as the greatest right-handed hitter in the history of the major leagues. But the Cardinals discovered him only because they were broke, and held onto him only because no one else wanted him.

At spring training in Texas in 1915, the club's lone scout, Bob Connery, was directed to scout only the lower rungs of the minor leagues. The team's owners told him that they didn't have the funds to sign any of the better prospects available and that he'd be wasting his time and their money by looking at blue-chip ballplayers. That spring, Connery was running the Cardinals "B" team, which played exhibition games around the state. When they stopped in the tiny town of Denison, the Class D team's skinny 18-year-old shortstop, Rogers Hornsby, made an impression. Though he batted only .232 the year before, Hornsby's attitude and demeanor, more than his physical gifts, impressed Connery. Years later, he recalled, "Contrary to reports, I was not too much impressed with Hornsby's hitting. What I saw was a loose, gangling kid with a good pair of hands, a strong arm and a world of pep and life on the field." Connery kept tabs on Hornsby during the season and that August, purchased his contract for $500.

In September, with the Cardinals near the bottom of the standings, Manager Miller Huggins brought Hornsby up for the final month of the season. In 18 games at shortstop, the 140-pound Hornsby hit .246 with only two extra base hits. When the eager young Hornsby asked Huggins his opinion, the manager told him he was too small for the major leagues and needed more time in the minors. Disappointed with their investment, the Cardinals offered to sell Hornsby to the Little Rock club for what they paid for him — $500. Little Rock refused. The Cardinals were stuck with Hornsby.

The following spring, Hornsby showed up in camp looking like a new man. He spent the off-season on his father's farm, working in the fields and drinking a quart of milk a day. He had added 30 pounds of muscle to his frame. He also proved a willing pupil in the batter's box. When Huggins suggested Hornsby would gain more power by abandoning his crouch and standing upright at the plate, Hornsby obliged. The results were immediate. Hornsby began spraying line drives all over the field. That spring, injuries to other shortstops gave Hornsby a chance to play every day. When spring training ended, Hornsby went north with the club and by the end of the 1916 season, he had hit for a .313 average. For a team that again finished in a tie for last place, Cardinals fans finally had a reason for optimism.

Branch Rickey
Executive, 1917 - 1942
Manager, 1919 - 1925

Branch Rickey presided over the golden age of Cardinals baseball. His 25-year tenure with the team was highlighted by a string of World Series titles and Hall of Fame caliber players. Rickey's impact on the Cardinals, and major league baseball, cannot be overstated. He was an innovator, a brilliant judge of talent, a shrewd negotiator and responsible for some of the most far-reaching changes the game ever saw.

Rickey played baseball in college, and briefly, in the major leagues. When an arm injury ended his career, he pursued a law degree while coaching baseball at the University of Michigan. In 1913, Rickey came to St. Louis in the front office of the Cardinals' cross-town rival, the St. Louis Browns. Named manager of the lowly Browns with 12 games left in the season, Rickey began putting his coaching theories into practice. His college background convinced him that baseball could be taught, with strict rules and procedures. Although Rickey lifted the Browns to a fifth-place finish in 1915, his law degree and business acumen proved of far greater value off the field.

By 1917, the new owners of the Cardinals were looking for a front office executive and lured Rickey away from the Browns. Following a short stint in Europe during World War I, Rickey returned to the Cardinals in time to start the 1919 season. He signed a three-year contract as manager and president, purchased 10 percent of the club's stock and set about rebuilding the franchise.

Rickey soon realized that the cash-strapped Cardinals couldn't compete with the contracts offered players by more successful clubs. He was forced to rely on contacts from his days as a college coach. He signed dozens of amateur players for little or no money and began stockpiling players. But his greatest coup was signing a series of working agreements with various minor league clubs. For decades, these independent clubs had made money by selling their best players to major league teams. Rickey changed all that. For a modest annual payment, Rickey and the Cardinals obtained the rights to purchase the contracts of hundreds of players, often at reduced prices. The result was an almost endless pool of available talent at very little cost. Within a decade, the Cardinals had so many players under contract, that the team purchased dozens of minor league clubs so that they had enough places for their prospects to play. This arrangement became so successful that by the early 1940s, the Cardinals owned more than two dozen minor league clubs.

The development of a "farm system" was only one of Rickey's many far-reaching innovations. On the field, he put in place a system of coaching instructions that was taught throughout the Cardinals' system. He introduced batting cages, sliding pits, mechanized pitching machines and later, in Pittsburgh, the batting helmet.

With the arrival of a new owner, automobile dealer Sam Breadon in 1920, Rickey finally had a partner whose desire to win was as strong as his own. Under their tenure, the Cardinals won six NL pennants and four World Series.

Austin McHenry
Outfielder, 1918 - 1922

Austin McHenry's splendid career was cut short by tragedy.

McHenry was a defensive outfielder with excellent speed and a rifle arm. Promoted to the Cardinals at age 22, McHenry quickly became an everyday player in the outfield. In 1919, he hit .286 and led the team with 19 doubles. In 1921, he hit .350 and drove in 102 runs, both third best in the league. Only the exploits of teammate Rogers Hornsby kept McHenry from being recognized as the Cardinals' best player.

However, early the next spring, McHenry began having trouble judging fly balls. He told manager Branch Rickey that his vision was failing. Sent for a medical exam, doctors at first found nothing wrong with McHenry. When rest failed to improve his condition, a decision was made to do exploratory surgery. Doctors discovered a brain tumor and McHenry learned his condition was fatal. By Thanksgiving, Austin McHenry was dead. He was 27 years old.

Bobby Wallace
Shortstop, 1899 - 1901; 1917 - 1918

Star shortstop Bobby Wallace spent more than 20 seasons playing in St. Louis, but not all of them with the Cardinals.

After moving with the Cardinals from Cleveland in 1899, Wallace batted .302 his first season and drove in 108 RBI, fifth best in the league. In 1901, he batted .322 and led the team in doubles and RBI.

But the rival American League, formed in 1901, began luring star players with huge salary offers. In 1902, the upstart league came after Wallace. Already making the National League's maximum annual salary of $2,400, Wallace was offered a five-year contract worth $32,000 to play for the Cardinals' cross-town rivals, the Browns. The Cardinals could have matched the offer, but decided to let the 28-year-old Wallace go.

Wallace spent parts of the next 15 years anchoring the Browns' infield. His quickness and range quickly established him as the new league's best shortstop. Only Honus Wagner in the National League was considered his equal. Distraught Cardinals fans often attended Browns games and pleaded with Wallace to return to their team. Over the years, Wallace's batting average slowly declined and by 1912, injuries kept him from playing every day.

In 1915, Wallace became an American League umpire for parts of two seasons before finally re-joining the Cardinals in 1917 at the age of 43. He played 40 games and batted just .148 before retiring. Wallace then managed in the minor leagues and coached in the majors with the Cincinnati Reds, for whom he scouted for the next 30 years. Bobby Wallace was elected to the Hall of Fame in 1953. He died in 1960.

Rogers Hornsby
Robison Field, 1918

By 1917, Rogers Hornsby had become the Cardinals' most dangerous offensive weapon. He batted a robust .327, second highest in the National League, hit 24 doubles and led the league in triples.

In 1919, when he hit .318, Hornsby became the hottest commodity in the league and the object of other teams' desires. As early as 1917, the Chicago Cubs had offered the Cardinals $75,000 for the everyday shortstop. The New York Giants, led by fiery manager John McGraw, also made repeated attempts to secure Hornsby. In 1919, the offer stood at $130,000. By 1921, after Hornsby had won two straight batting titles, the offer increased to a staggering $300,000, but the Cardinals refused to part with their star player.

But Hornsby was becoming belligerent and resentful of authority. He repeatedly clashed with manager Branch Rickey and on at least two occasions, the two had to be separated in the clubhouse. Hornsby's outspoken demeanor and caustic personality also rubbed his teammates the wrong way. Hornsby couldn't understand why his advice to others didn't produce the same results. Hornsby neither smoke nor drank, a rarity among players of his era. He even refused to read newspapers or attend movies for fear it would affect his batting eye. But his hitting lifted the Cardinals in the standings and in 1922, he gave Cardinals fans a season to remember.

Sam Breadon
Owner, 1920 - 1947

Businessman Sam Breadon's tenure as owner represented the golden age of Cardinals baseball. A self-made millionaire, Breadon's business acumen helped transform the team from perennial cellar-dwellers into a dynasty. His willingness to take a gamble and his penchant for winning earned him the nickname "Lucky Sam." The pairing of Breadon and Branch Rickey proved an unbeatable combination and was responsible for firmly establishing the Cardinals as a model for National League franchises. During Breadon's ownership, St. Louis won nine pennants and six World Series titles.

Sam Breadon was raised in New York City. In 1903, at the age of 23, he left his job as a bank clerk, took a $50 cut in his monthly pay and followed a friend to St. Louis to help run an automobile garage. But when the outgoing Breadon began talking to the garage's customers about opening his own operation, he was summarily fired. With the approach of the 1904 World's Fair in St. Louis, he convinced a local candy maker to advance him 30 cases of popcorn. He hired a dozen boys to sell his wares along the fair's parade route and made $35 for a single day's work. The re-sale of a second-hand car soon netted him another $200. These tiny profits allowed Breadon to enter a partnership with a socialite, Marion Lambert, a former client at the garage. With Lambert's financial backing, they formed The Western Automobile Company and were awarded one of the city's first Ford franchises. The company made $20,000 its first year and Breadon never looked back.

In 1917, Breadon was persuaded to invest in a stock offering from the struggling St. Louis Cardinals baseball club. He grudgingly bought four shares for $200. Over the next several seasons, Breadon loaned the club $18,000 to keep them afloat and by 1920, he was the team's largest stockholder. He reluctantly became president of the club, primarily to look after his financial interests. With Branch Rickey handling on-field affairs, Breadon's first move was to get the club out of their ballpark, the rapidly crumbling Robison Field, where they had played since 1899. He convinced the St. Louis Browns to let the Cardinals use their stadium, Sportsman's Park, when the Browns were out of town. For an annual payment of $25,000, the Cardinals had a new home. No longer in need of Robison Field, Breadon sold the land to the St. Louis Board of Education and the local transit authority for $275,000. This windfall put the franchise on solid financial ground, allowed the club to pay off all debts and left money for the signing of minor-league players. Sam Breadon and the Cardinals were on their way.

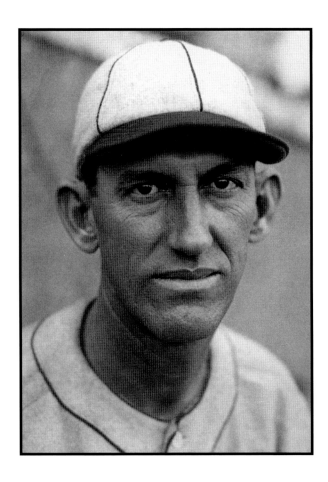

Miguel "Mike" Gonzalez
Catcher, 1915 - 1918; 1924 - 1925; 1931 - 1932

Cuban-born Mike Gonzalez parlayed his defensive skills into a lifetime career in the majors.
Gonzalez spent three stints with the Cardinals and all but three of his 17 major-league seasons as a back-up catcher. He had a strong arm, but swung a weak bat. In the three seasons that he played every day, he never hit above .262. Traded to the Giants in 1919, Gonzalez played only 72 games over three years before re-joining the Cardinals in 1924. Traded to the Cubs in 1925, Gonzalez backed up future Hall of Fame catcher Gabby Hartnett for five years. In 1932, at age 41, Gonzalez hung up his mitt and embarked on a second career as a coach with St. Louis. Twice, he served as interim manager for the Cardinals in 1938 and 1940. Later, his ownership of the Havana ball club in his native Cuba made him a national hero there.

Jack Smith
Outfielder, 1915 - 1926

Jack Smith was an everyday player in the major leagues by age 20. A speedy outfielder with a good arm, he stole 203 bases in 10 full seasons with St. Louis. His best years were 1920-23, when he hit .310 or better for four straight seasons. But by 1925, Smith was no longer an everyday player and the arrival of Chick Hafey made him expendable. The club sold Smith to the Boston Braves one game into the 1926 season. A back-up player for four seasons in Boston, Smith excelled in his role as a pinch-hitter. He spent two final seasons in the minors before retiring after the 1930 season. He later returned to the Chicago area and worked as a security guard for 25 years with the International Harvester Company.

Milt Stock
Third baseman, 1919 - 1923

Milt Stock was the finest third baseman in the early years of the Cardinals franchise. He was a superb contact hitter who rarely struck out. And he solidified the "hot corner," a position that saw a constant turnover of players prior to his arrival in 1919.

Unlike other third basemen of his day, Stock played an unusually deep third base, poised to snare possible doubles down the line. His speed allowed him to charge quickly for the occasional bunt. In his five seasons with St. Louis, Stock hit over .300 four times. In 1921, he batted .319 and his 204 hits were second-best in the National League, behind only teammate Rogers Hornsby.

But when he held out in a contract dispute, the Cardinals traded Stock to the Brooklyn Dodgers. There, in 1925, he batted a career-high .328 with 202 hits, including a streak of 16 consecutive hits over a four-game stretch. During an exhibition game in the spring of 1926, a collision with Yankees slugger Lou Gehrig effectively ended Stock's career. He spent the next five seasons as a player in the minors before serving as business manager for several minor-league clubs. In 1944, he returned to the majors and coached for eight seasons with the Cubs, Dodgers and Pirates.

George "Specs" Toporcer
Infielder, 1921 - 1928

"Specs" Toporcer's poor eyesight spurred his nickname and his legacy.

As a child, Specs didn't have time for baseball. His father died when Specs was 14, forcing the young boy to quit school and go to work.

As he grew, Specs began playing semi-pro ball on the sandlots of New York City, where he was spotted by a Cardinals scout who invited him to spring training in 1921. As it happened, veteran third baseman Milt Stock was a holdout that spring, allowing Specs, 22, a chance to show his stuff. Specs made the squad as a reserve player, but the holdout finally returned and the Cardinals sent Toporcer to their minor-league club in Syracuse. His stay there was short. After hitting .338 over a three-week period, Specs returned to St. Louis. In 1922, his only season as an everyday player, he hit .324. Over the next seven years, he was the Cardinals' super-sub, able to play any infield position with skill.

Sent to the minors in 1928, Specs was the leader on a team that won four straight International League titles. In 1929 and 1930, he was named the league's MVP. In 1932, he began managing in the minors. Later, he joined the Red Sox as a scout and eventually became director of the team's farm system.

But Toporcer's personal life was troubled. In 1945, his 16-year-old son died. Three years later, despite a series of operations, Specs lost the vision in his left eye. In 1951, while managing in Buffalo, he also lost the sight in his right eye, ending his career in baseball. His wife taught him to use a typewriter, which he used to author two books on baseball fundamentals. His sister also taught him to play golf by describing the shot needed and wiggling the flag in the cup on the greens so he could judge the distance to the hole.

Through it all, Specs remained an eternal optimist, telling a reporter late in life, "I'm in love with life. After all, we see with our minds, rather than our eyes." Specs became a sought-after inspirational speaker on the lecture circuit.

Bill Sherdel
Pitcher, 1918 - 1930; 1932

Bill Sherdel was a left-handed pitcher with good control who helped lead the Cardinals to two World Series. But in both series, Sherdel lost both his starts.

When he came to St. Louis from Milwaukee in 1917, Sherdel, nicknamed "Wee Willie" for his slight build, threw only two pitches, a fastball and a curveball. But under the tutelage of manager Branch Rickey, Sherdel mastered a third pitch called his "slow ball," known today as a change-up. With it, Sherdel developed into one of the league's most consistent winners.

Used as both a starter and a reliever, Sherdel won 17 games in 1922, including three shut-outs. In 1925, his 15-6 record gave him the best winning percentage in the National League. But in the 1926 World Series against the Yankees, Sherdel lost two one-run games despite an ERA of 2.12.

During the championship season of 1928, Sherdel had the best year of his career. He led the Cardinals staff in innings pitched, ERA and wins, with 21. He was on the mound when the Cardinals beat Boston, 3-1, to clinch the pennant for St. Louis. But again, he lost both his starts in the World Series and the Yankees swept the Cardinals in four straight.

Early in 1930, the Cardinals traded the 32-year-old Sherdel to the Boston Braves for veteran pitcher Burleigh Grimes. It proved a great trade for St. Louis as Grimes went 30-15 in a season and a half of work. Sherdel, on the other hand, went just 12-15 for Boston. Released by the Braves in 1932, Sherdel returned to pitch three games for St. Louis before retiring.

"Sunny Jim" Bottomley
First baseman, 1922 - 1932

James LeRoy Bottomley was a smooth-fielding first baseman who swung a powerful bat.

At the height of his career, Bottomley drove in at least 110 runners a year for six straight seasons. On September 16, 1924, he went six for six against Brooklyn and drove in a career-high 12 runs in a single game. Teammate Frankie Frisch called Bottomley "the greatest clutch hitter" he ever saw.

Bottomley could also hit for average. He was a lifetime .310 hitter and twice hit better than .365 with the Cardinals. In 1925, he led the National League in hits and doubles. The next year, he led the league in doubles and RBI. During the 1926 World Series against the Yankees, he batted .345 and his 10 hits tied for tops on the team.

In 1928, when the Cardinals won their second pennant in three years, Bottomley was chosen the league's Most Valuable Player. It was a popular choice. A soft-spoken country boy from rural Illinois, Bottomley's easy-going manner made him a favorite of teammates and fans alike. His nickname was "Sunny Jim."

In 1930, a thumb injury robbed Bottomley of his power and his production fell off dramatically. In 1933, he was traded to the Cincinnati Reds. Three years later, he returned to St. Louis, but this time with the Cardinals' cross-town rivals, the Browns. There, he batted .298 in his last season as a regular before managing the Browns for the second half of the 1937 season.

Bottomley twice managed in the minors for a single season, but then retired to his Illinois farm, where he enjoyed hunting and fishing. He was named to the Hall of Fame in 1974.

Ray Blades
Outfielder, 1922 - 1928; 1930 - 1932
Manager, 1939 - 1940

Ray Blades was a reserve outfielder whose playing career was cut short by injuries.

Blades was one of the first amateur players signed by Branch Rickey, who saw him play an exhibition game against the Cardinals in 1920. Sent to the minors, the scrappy Blades had a temper and developed a reputation for fighting.

Blades came to St. Louis in 1922 and two years later, became an everyday player. In 1925, he hit .342, including 37 doubles, but his aggressive play almost ended his career.

In the 1926 championship season, Blades ran headlong into the outfield wall at Sportsman's Park while attempting to field a long fly ball. His spikes caught in the wire screen lining the wall and he tore up his left knee, ending his season. Surgery left him with a limp and he was never an everyday player again. Sent to the minors in 1929, Blades battled back and spent another three years as a reserve with the Cardinals before retiring after the 1932 season.

At age 35, Blades began managing in the Cardinals' minor-league system. In his first season, he led the Columbus Redbirds to the American Association title with 101 wins. Six years later, in 1939, Blades was named to replace Frankie Frisch as manager of the Cardinals. By then, most of the team's star players were aging and the Cardinals hadn't won a pennant since 1934. Paced by a great year from slugger Johnny Mize, the Cardinals battled to win 92 games and finished second to the Cincinnati Reds. But the next year, the team got off to a 15-25 start and with the team in seventh place, Blades was replaced as manager by Billy Southworth. Blades managed in the minors for another five years before spending eight seasons as a coach with several major league teams.

Rogers Hornsby
Infielder, 1915 - 1926

In the history of the major leagues, only one player has ever hit at least 40 home runs while batting over .400 in the same season. Rogers Hornsby's .401 batting average and 42 home runs in 1922 ranks among the greatest hitting feats of all time. His 250 hits that season remain the Cardinals' all-time single-season record. He also led the National League in doubles, runs scored and slugging percentage. And his 152 RBI rank second only to Joe Medwick's 154 in 1937.

Hornsby was 26 in 1922, the first of two Triple Crown seasons. After having played several infield positions, he took over at second base in 1920 and the stability seemed to agree with his batting average. That season, he won his first batting title with a .370 average and led the league in hits, doubles and RBI. In 1921, he batted .397 and led the league in every offensive category except home runs. The two dominating seasons were a great build-up to 1922.

Although he would be named the league's MVP in 1925 and 1929, Hornsby's 1922 season remains one for the record books.

Taylor Douthit
Outfielder, 1923 - 1931

Taylor Douthit (pronounced dow-thit) was an exceptionally gifted outfielder who could run down anything hit his way.

Raised in Oakland and signed by the Cardinals out of the University of California, Douthit joined the Cardinals for a late look in the 1923 season and became an everyday player in 1926. Installed as the team's lead-off hitter, Douthit hit .308 and stole 23 bases to help the Cardinals win the National League pennant that year.

In 1929, Douthit batted a career-high .336 and notched 206 hits. When he racked up another 201 hits in 1930, he became just the third Cardinal in the 20th Century to achieve back-to-back 200-hit seasons. As of 2002, only eight Cardinals players had accomplished this feat.

Even more than his power at the plate, Douthit became best known for his mastery of the outfield, consistently snagging balls that should have meant hits and runs for opposing players. Twice he led NL outfielders in put-outs.

But in 1931, the Cardinals wanted to make room for a rookie outfielder named John "Pepper" Martin and Douthit was traded to the Reds. Douthit's batting average dropped each of the next three seasons and an arthritic hip forced him to retire after the 1933 season. He returned to Oakland and entered the insurance business.

Tommy Thevenow
Shortstop, 1924 - 1928

Tommy Thevenow's glove got him to the major leagues and kept him there for parts of 15 seasons, despite his injuries.

While never a big hitter, he came on strong in the 1926 postseason. In the World Series against the Yankees, he led all hitters with a .417 average and his clutch hit in Game 7 gave the Cardinals a 3-2 victory and secured the title. The following June, however, he broke his leg sliding into second base and missed the rest of the season. When he hit a lowly .205 in 1928, he spent most of the season on the bench.

Despite his weak bat, Thevenow was so highly valued for his defense that the Phillies paid the Cardinals $50,000 for him prior to the 1929 season. But during spring training, he was critically injured in an auto accident and missed a third of the season. Finally healthy, he returned to have his best year in 1931, batting .286 and playing in every game for the last-place Phillies. That year, he led all NL shortstops in put-outs and double plays. But he couldn't seem to avoid serious injury. Traded to Pittsburgh in 1931, he again broke his leg sliding into second.

By age 28, injuries had robbed most of his range and over the next seven seasons, he was used primarily as a reserve infielder. When he retired in 1938, he managed one season in the minors before returning to Indiana to run a grocery store.

Roscoe "Wattie" Holm
Outfielder, 1924 - 1929; 1932

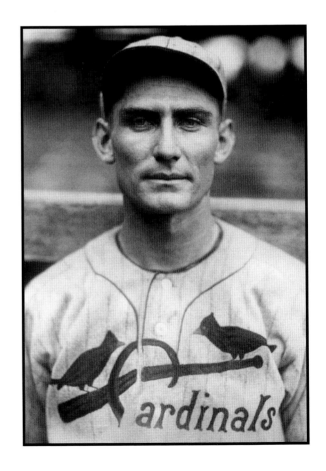

"Wattie" Holm's career ended because of an arm injury. His life ended because of a nagging headache and a gun.

During his seven seasons in baseball, all with the Cardinals, Holm moved around the diamond as a reserve. On occasion, he was sent to the minors.

The team signed Holm after he briefly attended the University of Iowa, where he had studied to be a dentist. But early in 1925, he twice fractured his leg and missed almost the entire season. The next year, he hit .285 but was used sparingly by new manager Rogers Hornsby. When he finally saw regular action in 1927, he hit a career high .286 and added 22 doubles. And in 1928, he hit a career-high three home runs, including a pinch-hit grand slam.

Sent to the minors in 1930, Holm returned to the Cardinals in 1932 for 11 games before a bad arm forced him to retire for good. Holm returned to Iowa, where he ran a sporting goods store for many years and coached the local semi-pro team. In 1950, he began complaining of constant head pains. A trip to the Mayo Clinic was inconclusive. Upset over his failing health, Holm fatally shot his wife and then himself. He was 49.

Jesse "Pop" Haines
Pitcher, 1920 - 1937

Jesse Haines was a three-time 20-game winner for St. Louis and the first Cardinals pitcher to throw a no-hitter in the 20th Century.

Before joining the Cardinals at age 27, Haines spent six years in the minor leagues. After watching him win 21 games for Kansas City in 1919, General Manager Branch Rickey scraped together $10,000 to bring him to St. Louis.

His first year with the Cardinals, Haines became the workhorse of the staff. He led the team in innings pitched and led the league in appearances. He pitched a 17-inning complete game against the Cubs that included 10 straight no-hit innings, although he eventually lost the game, 3-2. Despite throwing four shut-outs, his rookie year in St. Louis ended with a disappointing 13-20 record.

The next year, Haines led the staff with 18 wins and in 1923, he won 20 games for the first time. In the middle of 1924, the worst season of his career, Haines threw a masterpiece. On July 17 at Sportsman's Park, Haines no-hit the Boston Braves for a 5-0 victory. It was the first no-hitter by a Cardinals pitcher in almost 50 years and the highlight of a season in which he won just eight games.

After the Cardinals won the pennant in 1926, Haines was at his best in the World Series against the Yankees. He threw a complete-game shut-out and even hit a home run to win Game 3. He also was the winning pitcher in Game 7 after teammate Grover Cleveland Alexander threw three innings of scoreless relief.

Haines had his best season in 1927, when he won 24 games and led the league with six shut-outs and 25 complete games. The following year, at the age of 35, he led the Cardinals back to the World Series with another 20-win season.

On the mound, the quiet right-hander relied on the knuckleball. Unlike other pitchers of the day, he actually gripped the ball with his knuckles. He also developed a side-arm delivery that caused the ball to drop away from hitters, similar to a curveball. The pitch prolonged his career. In the 1930 World Series against the Philadelphia Athletics, Haines baffled opposing hitters for nine innings and threw a complete-game four-hitter to win Game 4.

Injuries kept Haines out of the 1931 Series and by 1932, he was used primarily out of the bullpen. When he retired at age 44 in 1937, he had 210 victories and 209 complete games. He ranks second on the Cardinals' all-time win list, behind Bob Gibson. Haines was elected to the Hall of Fame in 1970.

Charles "Flint" Rhem
Pitcher, 1924 - 1932; 1934; 1936

Flint Rhem was a 20-game winner during the Cardinals' 1926 championship season, but he is best remembered for an off-field incident late in 1930.

Rhem joined the Cardinals with much fanfare. His first year in the minors, he had struck out 282 batters in 293 innings, the most of any professional pitcher that season. He was promoted to the majors late that year, but saw limited action before making the starting rotation in 1925. Despite winning only eight games, Rhem developed an over-hand curveball to compliment his blazing fastball. In 1926, the big right-hander harnessed his arsenal of pitches and went 20-6, tops on the staff. He was chosen to pitch Game 4 of the World Series, but lasted only four innings, giving up two mammoth home runs to Babe Ruth in a game the Yankees won, 10-5.

The following spring, Rhem held out in a salary dispute. When he finally joined the team, he won his first two starts, but a sore arm limited him to a 10-12 record. Rhem was unable to re-gain his championship form over the next three seasons, winning a high of 12 games in 1930. Late that season, with the Cardinals chasing the Dodgers for the National League pennant, St. Louis arrived in New York for a key series with Brooklyn. Like most players of his era, Rhem enjoyed a drink and was a constant companion of Cardinals pitcher Grover Cleveland Alexander, himself a heavy drinker. With Rhem scheduled to pitch the next day at Ebbetts Field, the two players hit the town. The next morning, Rhem couldn't get out of bed. He didn't appear at the ballpark for two days. A story appeared in the papers claiming that Rhem had been kidnapped at gunpoint, driven to New Jersey, tied up and forced to drink whiskey until too drunk to pitch.

For years, Rhem claimed the story was true. Finally, in an interview in 1961, he admitted the story was made up. He'd been too sick to pitch, then holed up in his hotel room. Rhem claimed that general manager Branch Rickey had come to his room and, with a group of reporters outside, helped spread the word of his "kidnapping."

Rhem was traded to the Phillies during the 1932 season. Twice, he briefly returned to the Cardinals before retiring after the 1936 season. Rhem returned to run the family farm in South Carolina until his death in 1969 at the age of 68.

Charles "Chick" Hafey
Outfielder, 1924 - 1931

Chick Hafey is one of the greatest right-handed hitters of all time. "He doesn't hit line drives. That's chain lightening that leaves his bat," noted New York Giants' third baseman Freddie Lindstrom, himself a future Hall of Famer.

The Cardinals signed Hafey at 19, and converted him from pitcher to outfielder because of his hot bat and strong arm. Teammate Ernie Lombardi had great respect for Hafey's natural talent. "Once in a pre-game throwing contest, he threw a ball from home plate over the left-field fence in Cincinnati. That fence was then 330 feet away and about 25 feet high. I don't think there's anyone around today with that kind of arm."

Hafey's achievements were even more amazing considering his recurring health problems. In 1926, he complained of headaches and blurred vision. He told reporters, "If I closed my right eye, I couldn't see thirty feet." Doctors diagnosed chronic sinus infections. A series of operations failed to provide relief and Hafey's vision further deteriorated. And yet, starting in 1927, he began the five greatest seasons of his career. That year, he batted .329 and led the National League in slugging percentage. Along with roommate Jim Bottomley, he became one of the Cardinals' most consistent run producers. He had three straight years with more than 100 RBI and four consecutive seasons when his batting average never dipped below .336. In 1931, he won the league's batting crown with a .349 average.

Off the field, Hafey and General Manager Branch Rickey sparred over the terms of his contract. In 1931, Rickey deducted $2,100 from Hafey's annual salary of $12,500 because he missed most of spring training with medical problems. After Hafey won a batting title that season, he arrived in camp the following spring expecting a significant raise. Rickey offered him another $500. Hafey was so insulted that he immediately left camp and drove back home to California. Rickey traded him to the Cincinnati Reds three weeks later. There, he got a $15,000 salary, but was saddled with a last-place team. Injuries cost him half of the 1932 season and his sinus problems grew worse. His power numbers dropped dramatically and he missed almost two entire seasons. By 1935, no longer an everyday player, he retired. After a brief comeback in 1937, he returned to his ranch in California.

In 1971, Hafey was elected to the Hall of Fame. He died two years later at age 70.

Frankie Frisch and Rogers Hornsby
Polo Grounds, 1926

At the time this picture was taken, neither Frankie Frisch nor Rogers Hornsby could know that at season's end, they would be switching teams in the biggest trade of the decade.

By 1926, Hornsby had won six consecutive National League batting titles and was about to lead the Cardinals to their first ever World Series title. Frisch was a superb second baseman and an excellent hitter for the New York Giants, but couldn't match Hornsby's gaudy power stats.

But friction between Hornsby and Cardinals' owner Sam Breadon heated up as the season neared its end. In last place when Hornsby was named manager early in the season, the Cardinals were fighting for the pennant when they took an eastern road-trip in September. Breadon, always hunting for additional revenue, scheduled the Cardinals to play an exhibition game in New Haven on an off day. When Hornsby learned of the game, he berated Breadon in the clubhouse. He accused the owner of caring more about money than about having his team well rested for the stretch.

After the Cardinals won the pennant and defeated the Yankees to win the World Series, the owner and manager sat down to discuss Hornsby's new contract. Hornsby had made $30,000 in 1925 and 1926. Having just won the championship, he wanted a three-year contract that paid $50,000 a year. Breadon countered with a one-year deal. A stalemate ensued. On December 20, 1926, Breadon announced that he had traded Hornsby to the Giants for Frisch and veteran pitcher Jimmy Ring.

Cardinals fans were outraged. They hung black crepe on the doors and windows at Breadon's residence and at his auto dealership. The local newspapers ran editorials questioning his sanity. But there was little they could do. Hornsby was gone. Breadon answered his critics saying, "I came to the decision that if I was president, my chief must work with me. If he didn't, either he or I must get out, and I wasn't ready to leave the club."

Bob O'Farrell
Catcher, 1925 - 1928; 1933; 1935
Manager, 1927

After the Cardinals traded World Series-winning manager Rogers Hornsby, Branch Rickey picked Bob O'Farrell to manage the team in 1927.

O'Farrell was a veteran catcher who'd had his greatest season during the team's championship run. He'd come from Chicago in 1925, having twice led National League catchers in games played. But a fractured skull in 1924 and the emergence of catcher "Gabby" Hartnett made him expendable to the Cubs.

Never a big offensive threat, O'Farrell was known more for an accurate throwing arm and his masterful handling of a pitching staff. He caught 147 of 154 games for the Cardinals in 1926. Surprisingly, he also came through big at the plate. He batted .293 with 30 doubles and 68 RBI. O'Farrell was the almost unanimous choice as the league's Most Valuable Player. In the World Series, he batted .304 and threw out Babe Ruth as he attempted to steal second. The throw ended Game 7 and secured the series.

A broken thumb the following spring meant he could no longer play every day. And so, splitting time with "Pancho" Snyder behind the plate, he managed the Cardinals to a 92-61 record, an improvement of three and a half games over 1926. Unfortunately, the Pittsburgh Pirates won 94 games and the pennant. The Cardinals' management, spoiled by wining it all in 1926, fired O'Farrell at season's end. Traded to the New York Giants in 1928, O'Farrell spent five seasons as backup for manager John McGraw. He returned to the Cardinals briefly in 1933 and again in 1935, before finally retiring at age 40. He managed in the minors for one season, before spending the next three decades owning and operating a bowling alley in his hometown of Waukegan, Illinois.

Les Bell
Infielder, 1923 - 1927

Third baseman Les Bell played all but one game during the 1926 championship season, batting a team-high .325, with 17 home runs and 100 RBI.

Bell's knack for clutch hits included a 23-game hitting streak as the Cardinals, in fifth place at the beginning of June, surged past four teams to capture their first National League pennant. In Brooklyn on September 22, Bell hit three triples and a double as the Cards romped 15-7. Two days later, St. Louis clinched.

But Bell's offensive production fell badly in 1927 when he hit just .259. He was traded to Boston, where he rejoined former teammate Rogers Hornsby, now playing for the Braves. Bell rebounded to drive in 91 runs for a seventh-place team that lost 103 games. Traded to the Cubs in 1930, Bell served as a backup for two seasons before spending another two years playing in the minors.

In 1940, Bell began a second career as a minor-league manager, a job he held for 10 years. He retired to his native Harrisburg, Pa., to run an amateur baseball program for the city parks department.

Billy Southworth
Outfielder, 1926 - 1927; 1929
Manager, 1929

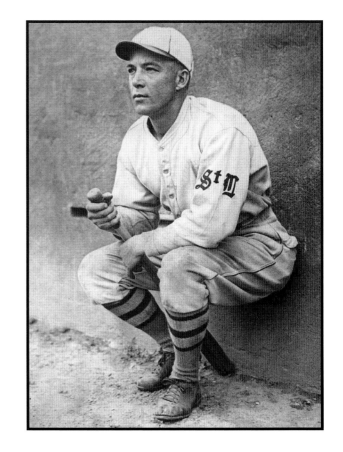

Hustling Billy Southworth spent nearly 40 years as a player and manager in professional baseball. The talented veteran came to the Cardinals from the New York Giants midway through the 1926 season and made an immediate impact. He hit .317 with 11 home runs and 69 RBI while holding down the right-field job. It was his two-run home run on September 24 against the Giants that clinched the pennant for St. Louis.

In that fall's World Series, he was even better. Southworth led the team with a .345 average and his three-run homer won Game 2. In addition, his diving circus catch of a Yankee line drive, which he turned into a double play, snuffed out a rally in Game 6 and preserved the Cardinals' victory. But a rib injury cost him almost half the 1927 season. In 1928, Southworth was named player-manager of the Cardinals' top farm club at Rochester.

His first year in Rochester, Southworth led the team to the International League title. Halfway through the 1929 season, with the team in first place, he was called to St. Louis to replace Cardinals manager Bill McKechnie, whose team was in fourth place. Despite the switch, the Cardinals finished fourth and Southworth was fired, too. He returned to Rochester and won two consecutive championships in 1930 and 1931. It would be another nine years before he again managed in the major leagues.

**Sam Breadon, a family friend, Mrs. Breadon, Mrs. Hornsby and Rogers Hornsby
1926 World Series**

Rogers Hornsby, who led St. Louis to the 1926 World Series title and then was traded to the New York Giants following a contract dispute, exacted his revenge against Cardinals owner Sam Breadon four months later.

It took the form of financial revenge, one rooted in the deal that Hornsby struck when he first became manager of the Cardinals.

Hornsby had been allowed to purchase outgoing manager Branch Rickey's 1,167 shares of stock for $45 each. But now that Hornsby was a member of the Giants, Commissioner Kennesaw Mountain Landis ruled that no player could own stock in another team. Breadon was forced to buy it back.

Hornsby figured his stock was worth considerably more since the Cardinals had just won the championship. He demanded $100 per share.

Breadon was outraged, but was forced to pay up. In April 1927, with help from the other seven National League owners, Breadon put together $116,700 and met Hornsby's price.

Grover Cleveland Alexander
Pitcher, 1926 - 1929

By the time Grover Cleveland Alexander arrived in St. Louis, he was 39 years old and had won 318 major-league games. Eight times he'd won at least 20 games in a season. Three times, he'd won at least 30.

A record crowd of 37,000-plus turned out at Sportsman's Park to cheer Alexander's first start and watch him beat his former team, the Chicago Cubs, in 10 innings. The Cubs had let him go, tired of his constant drinking. Alexander suffered from epilepsy and claimed he drank to control the seizures he'd suffered since serving in an artillery unit in France during World War I.

The Cardinals picked up Alexander for the $6,000 waiver price and almost immediately, the big right-hander was back winning games.

His play in the 1926 World Series against the Yankees made Alexander a legend. In Game 2, Alexander evened the series by striking out 10 players and holding New York to four hits for a 6-2 Cardinals win. In Game 6, he threw a second complete game and easily won, 10-2, to again even the series. His pivotal moment came in Game 7. The Cardinals had rallied behind starter Jesse Haines to lead, 3-2, after six innings. But in the top of the seventh, the Yankees loaded the bases with two outs. Alexander was called from the bullpen, even though he had pitched nine innings the day before. Taking the mound, he assured Hornsby that he was up to the task. In the batter's box stood Tony Lazzeri, whose 114 RBI during the regular season were second only to Babe Ruth's. Four pitches later, Lazzeri had struck out and the inning was over. Alexander threw two more scoreless innings to give the Cardinals their first World Series title. The old man had done it. Remarkably, his ERA for the series was 0.89 and his 17 strike-outs led all pitchers.

In 1927, Alexander had his last great season, winning 21 games. He pitched for the Cardinals another two years before his drinking got him traded to the Phillies in 1930. He later spent several years barnstorming throughout the minors to make ends meet. Elected to the Hall of Fame in 1937, Alexander died alone and destitute in 1950.

Frankie Frisch
Second baseman, 1927 - 1937

Frankie Frisch faced the unenviable task of replacing Rogers Hornsby, a six-time batting champion and championship-winning manager, at second base in 1927. But in the end, Frisch's fiery personality and leadership on the field helped inspire the golden age of Cardinals baseball.

Frisch was a gifted, all-around athlete. At Fordham University, he'd played four sports and was nicknamed the "Fordham Flash" for his speed on the football field. He joined the New York Giants in 1919 without having played a single day in the minors. In New York, he honed his skills under the watchful eye of legendary Giants manager John McGraw, who alternated him between second and third base.

Frisch was a star by the age of 22. In 1921, his second full year in the majors, he helped the Giants win the pennant by hitting .341 and leading the league with 49 stolen bases. In 1923, he hit .348 and led the National League with 223 hits as the Giants won their third straight NL pennant. Frisch was a natural switch-hitter at the plate and his aggressive, scrappy style earned him the respect of players throughout the league.

In St. Louis, his debut was a rousing success. He batted .337 his first year, with 208 hits. He led the league with 48 stolen bases and played flawless defense. By a single vote, he finished second to Pittsburgh's Paul Waner for the NL's MVP award. Although the Cardinals failed to repeat as champions, it was through no fault of Frisch's.

Starting in 1928, the Cardinals returned to the World Series in three of the next four seasons. In 1930, Frisch batted .346 and his 114 RBI were tops on the team. In 1931, the Cardinals won more than 100 games for the first time in the century and Frisch was named the league's MVP. Frisch also has the distinction of hitting the first National League home run in an All-Star game in 1933, a feat he repeated in 1934. A consistent winner everywhere he played, Frisch won pennants in eight of his 16 seasons as an everyday player.

Ernie Orsatti
Outfielder, 1927 - 1935

Ernie Orsatti spent his entire nine-year career in the major leagues with the Cardinals, but was an everyday player for only four seasons.

As a young man growing up near the movie lots in southern California, he worked as a movie stunt man for silent comedian Buster Keaton. Keaton was the part owner of a minor league club in the Pacific Coast League and soon, Orsatti was signed to a professional contract. Spotted by Branch Rickey on a scouting trip in 1925, Orsatti spent the next three seasons bouncing back and forth between the minors and St. Louis before becoming the Cardinals' regular rightfielder in 1929.

His daredevil background made Orsatti a fearless outfielder. He ran into walls and made diving catches on balls hit into the gaps. He also was a personable fellow, who sometime Invited teammates over to eat gourmet meals he cooked himself. Along with Leo Durocher, Orsatti was considered the sharpest dresser on the Cardinals team.

Despite hitting over .300 in limited duty, Orsatti had trouble breaking into an outfield that featured veterans Chick Hafey, Taylor Douthit and, starting in 1931, Pepper Martin. The trade of Hafey to Cincinnati in 1932 finally opened an outfield spot for Orsatti and he saw regular action over the next three seasons. In the 1934 World Series, he batted .314. But the arrival of outfielder Terry Moore in 1935 spelled the end of the line for the 32-year-old Orsatti. He returned to California and worked as a talent agent in Hollywood before opening a floral shop.

Bill McKechnie
Manager, 1928 - 1929

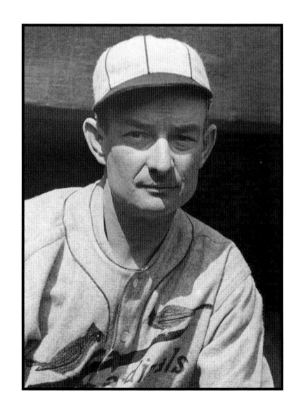

Bill McKechnie was a mediocre infielder during his 11 years in the major leagues, but his exceptional knowledge of the game made him a Hall of Fame manager. He is the only National League manager to win pennants with three different teams.

During his five seasons in Pittsburgh, the Pirates won the 1925 World Series and finished third three times. In 1927, the Cardinals hired him as a coach under new manager Bob O'Farrell and, when the team finished in second place, McKechnie was named manager for the 1928 season.

Like Cardinals General Manager Branch Rickey, McKechnie was a devoutly religious man. Rickey thought "the Deacon," as McKechnie was called, was the perfect man to lead the Cardinals back to the World Series. He was right. With Cardinals first baseman Jim Bottomley having an MVP year and a pitching staff that boasted two 20-game winners in Bill Sherdel and Jesse Haines, the Cardinals won the NL pennant in 1928. But in the World Series, the New York Yankees swept the Cardinals in four straight.

Cardinals owner Sam Breadon punished McKechnie by demoting him to manage the team's top minor-league club in Rochester. When his replacement, Billy Southworth, had the Cardinals in fourth place midway though the 1929 season, Breadon brought McKechnie back to finish out the season. Humiliated by the treatment, McKechnie was only too eager to accept an offer with another club.

In 1930, McKechnie took over the Boston Braves, one of the league's worst teams. Gradually, he lifted the Braves to fourth-place finishes in 1933 and 1934. It was considered a monumental turnaround for the hapless franchise and in 1937, he was named Manager of the Year. Lured away by the Cincinnati Reds in 1938, McKechnie won NL titles in 1939 and 1940. After nine seasons with the Reds, he became a coach with the Cleveland Indians for several seasons.

McKechnie was elected to the Hall of Fame in 1962.

Chick Hafey, Frankie Frisch, Jim Bottomley, George Harper
World Series, 1928

Four of the Cardinals' biggest bats posed for photographers before Game 1 of the 1928 World Series at Yankee Stadium.

During the season, Hafey had hit .337 with 27 home runs and 111 RBI, while Frisch had batted .300 and drove in 86 runs. Jim Bottomley's 31 homers and 136 RBI were both tops in the National League and earned him the league's MVP award. Rightfielder Harper had hit .305 with 17 home runs.

In the series, the Cardinals batters were no match for the Yankees pitchers. New York's three starters threw four complete games, struck out 29 batters and limited St. Louis to 10 runs. Conversely, Yankee sluggers Babe Ruth and Lou Gehrig hit a combined seven home runs as New York swept the series in four straight.

"Wild Bill" Hallahan
Pitcher, 1925 - 1926; 1929 - 1936

Bill Hallahan's fastball and lack of control earned him the nickname "Wild Bill."

Signed by the Cardinals at age 22, Hallahan's penchant for walking batters kept him in the minors for five seasons. Only after harnessing his pitches and winning 23 games for Houston in 1928 was he promoted to the Cardinals' staff. In St. Louis, manager Gabby Street corrected a flaw in Hallahan's delivery that allowed the 27-year-old to develop into one of the Cardinals' most effective starters. In 1930, he won 15 games and, true to his nickname, led the National League in strike-outs and walks.

As the 1930 season wound down, the Cardinals were trailing the Brooklyn Dodgers with two weeks left in the season. On September 16, Hallahan was forced into an emergency start after fellow Cardinals pitcher Flint Rhem turned up "missing." Hallahan shut out the Dodgers in 10 innings, besting Brooklyn's ace, Dazzy Vance, 1-0. The win put the Cardinals in first place and they never looked back. In the 1930 World Series against the Philadelphia Athletics, Hallahan threw a complete-game shut-out in Game 3, but the A's took the series in six games.

When the Cardinals repeated as NL champs in 1931, Hallahan led the way. He won 19 games, tops in the league. And true to form, for the second straight year, he led the league in strike-outs and walks. In a rematch against the Athletics in the World Series, Hallahan was overpowering. In Game 2, he evened the series by holding the A's to three hits and, despite seven walks and a wild pitch, he won, 2-0. In Game 5, he threw his second straight complete game, winning 5-1. Finally, with the series tied at three games, Hallahan preserved a 4-2 Cardinals victory in Game 7 by halting a late rally. His ERA for the series was a staggering 0.49. It was the high point of his career.

Over the next four seasons, Hallahan was a mediocre 41-40 for the Cardinals. He won 16 games in 1933, but characteristically led the league in walks. That same year, Hallahan was chosen as the National League's starting pitcher in the first-ever All-Star game. But early in 1936, the Cardinals sold Hallahan to the Reds, where he went 8-18 in two seasons of work. Signed by the Phillies in 1938, he went 1-8 in his last season in the majors. In 1939, Hallahan pitched five games in the minor leagues before retiring for good.

Jimmie Wilson
Catcher, 1928 - 1933

Catcher Jimmie Wilson was a career baseball man who spent more than two decades in the major leagues as a player, coach and manager.

Considered one of the finest signal-callers of his era, Wilson spent his first five seasons in the majors with his hometown Philadelphia Phillies. Although he batted over .300 twice, Wilson was traded to the Cardinals in 1928 for another catcher, Virgil "Spud" Davis. In St. Louis, Wilson's knowledge of opposing hitters and his quick glove soon made him a favorite of the Cardinals pitching staff.

At the plate, Wilson never showed much power. His highest home run total in a season was six. However, his slashing line drives produced a .325 average in 1929 and .318 the next year. In 1931, the Cardinals repeated as National League champs and Wilson finished sixth in the voting for league MVP. But the naming of Frankie Frisch as Cardinals manager midway through the 1933 season spelled the end for Wilson. He and Frisch didn't get along and Wilson was traded back to the Phillies, where he was named player-manager for the 1934 season.

In five seasons under Wilson, the hapless Phillies never finished higher than seventh. The losses wore on Wilson and he resigned following the 1938 season to become a coach with the Cincinnati Reds. In 1939, the Reds won the first of two straight NL crowns and Wilson found himself the unlikely hero of the 1940 World Series. At age 40, he was pressed into service, catching six of the series' seven games. Wilson batted .353 and stole the only base of the series as the Reds beat the Detroit Tigers in seven games. Wilson's sudden fame got him named manager of the Chicago Cubs in 1941. But the war-time Cubs were a sorry lot and when the team lost nine of its first 10 games in 1944, Wilson resigned. He returned to the Reds as a coach for two years before retiring to Florida in 1946. The following May, Wilson suffered a heart attack and died. He was 46.

Charlie Gelbert
Shortstop, 1929 - 1932; 1935 - 1936

Charlie Gelbert was a slick-fielding shortstop whose career was cut short by a hunting accident.

Signed by the Cardinals while still in college, Gelbert was a star in the minors. In 1928, his second year, he hit .340, drove in 116 runs and stole 30 bases for the farm club in Rochester. At age 23, he was named the Cardinals' everyday shortstop. Teamed with veteran second baseman Frankie Frisch, Gelbert blossomed into a superb fielder and hitter. In 1930, he hit .304 and rapped out 39 doubles. In that fall's World Series, he batted .353 and was the only Cardinals regular to hit over .275.

Following the 1932 season, Gelbert was at home in rural Pennsylvania hunting with some friends when he tripped and fell. His shotgun went off, discharging a load of buckshot into his left leg, just above the ankle. Doctors thought they might have to amputate the leg to save his life. The injury cost him two full seasons. When he returned to the Cardinals in 1935, his range was gone. Now a reserve, Gelbert spent two additional years with St. Louis before being traded to Cincinnati in 1937. Only 31, Gelbert bounced between five teams over the next four years before retiring after the 1941 season.

When World War II broke out, Gelbert enlisted in the Navy and served in the Pacific. In 1943, he returned to Pennsylvania and took over as baseball coach at Lafayette College. Over the next 23 seasons, his teams won 307 games and he was inducted into the Pennsylvania Sports Hall of Fame in 1966. The following January, Gelbert suffered a heart attack and died at the age of 60.

Syl Johnson
Pitcher, 1926 - 1933

Right-hander Syl Johnson spent 19 years pitching in the major leagues, but because of injuries, he won no more than 13 games in a single season.

Johnson pitched for the Detroit Tigers for four years until he was hit by a line drive that broke eight bones in his face. It took doctors seven days to re-open his left eye. When he recovered, Detroit sent him to the minor leagues, where the Cardinals signed him for the 1926 season.

Johnson couldn't seem to avoid batted balls or the injuries that came with them. His first year in St. Louis was cut short by a line drive that broke his big toe. When he returned, while pitching batting practice, a batted ball broke two of his ribs. Johnson was sent home for the remainder of the season and had to listen to the Cardinals' World Series on the radio. Sent to Rochester in 1927, he stayed healthy long enough to win 18 games and pitch a no-hitter.

In 1929, Johnson came back to the Cardinals and went 13-7. For the next three years, he was used as both a starter and a reliever. But he was generally ineffective and by 1932, he was pitching exclusively out of the bullpen. Following the 1933 season, he was traded to Cincinnati, where he pitched in only two games before being traded again, this time to the lowly Phillies. Johnson spent six seasons in Philadelphia before being released after the 1940 season. At age 40, he pitched another five years in the Pacific Coast League for Seattle before managing Vancouver for a single season in 1946. Johnson spent the next 15 years as a scout for the Yankees and Dodgers.

Charles "Gabby" Street
Manager, 1930 - 1933

Gabby Street was the first Cardinals manager to win consecutive National League pennants.

Street took over the team when Bill McKechnie left to manage the Boston Braves in 1930. As a former major-league catcher, Street came up from managing in the minors where he'd won two titles in nine seasons.

With his young players, Street stressed the fundamentals. With his veterans, he worked on conditioning. In mid-August, the fourth-place Cardinals rebounded from injuries and caught fire, winning 39 of their final 49 games. The team overtook the Chicago Cubs and won the pennant. But in the World Series, the powerful lineup of Connie Mack's Philadelphia Athletics proved too much. The Cardinals lost in six games.

In 1931, the Cardinals won 101 games and ran away with the pennant. The rematch against the Athletics, playing in their third straight World Series, was a much closer affair. The Cardinals' improved pitching proved the difference. Despite being outscored 22-19 in the series, the Cardinals won the decisive seventh game and "Ole Sarge," as Street was known from his military days, became the toast of St. Louis.

In 1932, however, the Cardinals never got in the race and finished sixth. By mid-season the following year, with the team in fifth place, Sam Breadon replaced Street with Frankie Frisch.

Street spent the next four years managing in the minors before returning to St. Louis in 1937 as a coach with the Browns. He piloted the Browns to a sixth-place finish in 1938 before retiring to his home in Joplin, Missouri. In 1945, he was lured back to St. Louis to team with broadcaster Harry Caray in the radio booth, one of the first ex-players to go behind the microphone. Together they spent the next five seasons entertaining listeners with their stories. Years later, Caray recalled, "He was a great talent. He was born 40 years too soon — today he'd be a national talent. He'd always have a humorous story to fit the situation on the field and he was a great baseball analyst." Early in 1951, Street lost his battle with cancer and died at the age of 68.

Earl "Sparky" Adams
Infielder, 1930 - 1933

At 5-foot-4 and 150 pounds, Sparky Adams was one of the smallest players ever to play in the major leagues.

He spent his first eight seasons with the Cubs and then the Pirates, where he led the National League in at-bats for three straight years. He stole at least 20 bases in four seasons.

When Adams joined the Cardinals in 1930, he was 35 and about to have the two finest years of his career. At third base, he led the league in fielding percentage for two years. In 1930, he batted a career-high .314 and the next year, his 46 doubles led the league.

Adams missed most of the 1931 World Series with a bad ankle and all but six weeks of the 1932 season with a knee injury. In 1933, he was traded, along with Paul Derringer, to the Reds for shortstop Leo Durocher. After two years in Cincinnati, he spent one more season in the minors before retiring in 1935. Adams returned to Pennsylvania where he turned to farming, then ran a service station. He died in 1989 at the age of 94.

Paul Derringer
Pitcher, 1931 - 1933

Paul Derringer won 223 games in the majors. Unfortunately for Cardinals fans, he won only 29 with St. Louis.

As a minor-leaguer in the Cardinals chain, Derringer won 40 games in two years with Rochester. His rookie year in St. Louis, the 24-year-old Derringer went 18-8 and threw four shutouts. But his erratic pitching in the World Series against Philadelphia and his streaks of wildness left management uncertain about the big right-hander. In 1932, Derringer went 11-14. In fairness to him, only Dizzy Dean won more than 12 games that season for the sixth-place Cardinals.

The next year, the Cardinals found themselves searching for a shortstop because of the hunting injury that felled Charlie Gelbert. Branch Rickey wanted Leo Durocher, then with Cincinnati. Durocher was a scrappy veteran known for his solid glove work. The cost: Derringer and infielder Sparky Adams.

The trade proved a steep price as Derringer eventually became the ace of the Cincinnati staff, a four-time 20-game winner and a four-time All-Star. With the Reds, Derringer would go on to win 154 games in nine full seasons and lead Cincinnati to National League pennants in 1939 and 1940.

John "Pepper" Martin
Outfielder, Third baseman; 1928; 1930 - 1940; 1944

John "Pepper" Martin knew only one way to play ball and live life — all out. His hustle on the field and his pranks on the road cast him as the ringleader of the Cardinals' famous "Gas House Gang."

Nicknamed "Pepper" for his aggressive style of play, Martin tore his way through the Cardinals' minor-league system. His strong arm and base-running speed matched his power at the plate.

The Cardinals made Martin an outfielder and brought him to St. Louis in 1928, but he spent most of the season on the bench. He was sent back to the minors for more seasoning and in Rochester, the 26-year-old had a monster year in 1930, batting .363 with 20 home runs and 114 RBI. The Cardinals' brass finally was convinced that Martin was ready for the big leagues.

But it was his flamboyant style off the field that caught the eye of sportswriters. As a young man in the minor leagues during the Depression, Martin preferred to save money by hopping a moving freight train each year to training camp in Florida. He would show up unshaven and grimy, looking like his traveling companions, the hobos.

In the off season, he raced midget stock cars. During the season, on the road, he delighted teammates with practical jokes. He dropped water balloons from hotel windows, put sneezing powder on ceiling fans in hotel lobbies and organized the team's first musical group, the "Mudcat Band," which sang off-key renditions of popular tunes.

Martin became a household name for his torrid play in the 1931 World Series. He batted .500 with four doubles and a homer, scoring five runs and driving in five others. On the base paths, Martin's head-first slides resulted in five stolen bases as he terrorized the Athletics' pitchers. The Cardinals won the series in seven games. For a nation mired in the Depression, the simple country boy with the colorful nickname proved an instant celebrity.

James "Ripper" Collins
First baseman, 1931 - 1936

Ripper Collins took over "Sunny Jim" Bottomley's spot at first base and became a fixture with the "Gas House Gang" Cardinals.

His first year in St. Louis, the 27-year-old rookie split time with the veteran Bottomley at first base and batted .301. In 1932, he led the team with 21 home runs and 91 RBI and made Bottomley expendable.

Though small for his position, Collins developed into the Cardinals' best run producer. In 1934, he hit .333 and drove in 128 runs. He also hit 35 home runs, tying the Giants' Mel Ott for most in the National League. In addition, Collins' 87 extra-base hits and 128 RBI remain the league's single-season record by a switch-hitter. It was the best season of his career and helped St. Louis win the pennant and a World Series title.

Although he was all business on the field, Collins, along with Pepper Martin, was a central figure in the players' off-field hi-jinks. During the 1936 season, in Philadelphia to play the Phillies, Collins, Martin and Dizzy Dean pulled one of their most notorious stunts. The team was staying at the posh Bellevue-Stratford Hotel when the players came across a cache of painters' gear. They quickly changed into the white coveralls, gathered up the paint cans, brushes and step ladders, and walked into the hotel ballroom where a luncheon banquet was underway. To the horror of the diners, the players began moving furniture, setting up their ladders and spreading tarps around the room. With Collins shouting foreman-like instructions, the players began attempting to slosh paint on the walls. When the hotel manager arrived and their true identities were uncovered, the luncheon guests were so impressed that the players were invited to sit at the head table and entertain the throng with their stories. Life was never dull on the road with the Gas House Gang.

In 1937, Collins was replaced at first base by another rookie, Johnny Mize, and traded to the Cubs. There, in his last season as an everyday player, he helped Chicago win the 1938 NL pennant. He spent the next two seasons in the Pacific Coast League before returning to the majors briefly in 1941 with the Pirates. In 1942, Collins became a player-manager in the minor leagues, where he was named the Eastern League MVP in 1944 for batting .396 at the age of 40. He later rejoined the Cubs as a coach in 1961 for three seasons.

Jay "Dizzy" Dean
Pitcher, 1930; 1932 - 1937

The only thing that moved faster than Dizzy Dean's fastball was his mouth, spurred by his penchant for self-promotion.

Dean joined St. Louis late in 1930 after winning 25 games by September his first year in the minors. The 20-year-old rookie joined the Cardinals the day after the team clinched the 1930 National League pennant. He started — and won — the final game of the season.

As his teammates left town for the World Series in Philadelphia, Dean returned home and told local reporters, "Show me another pitcher in the majors who has never been defeated. I told Mr. Rickey I would wait until next year and win him three games in the World Series. Don't think that I'm bragging about all this, I'm just letting you in on some inside facts. Oh yeah, next year I'm going to be known as the Great Dean."

When Dean reported to camp the next spring, manager Gabby Street was put off by his attitude. Dean frequently overslept and missed the team's 10 a.m. practice. He began running up charges at local stores and expected the team to pay the bills. The team warned merchants not to extend him credit and put Dean on a $1 daily allowance.

There was no denying his immense talent, but Dean was vying for a spot on a veteran team that had won the pennant the year before. Two weeks into the 1931 season, without ever pitching a single inning, Dean was sent to the team's Houston farm club.

In Houston, Dean met his future wife, Pat, whom he married after a six-week courtship. Marriage settled him down and he put together a remarkable season. He led the Texas League with 26 wins, a 1.57 ERA and 303 strike-outs.

Dean's success in the minors got him into the Cardinals' rotation for the 1932 season. On June 26, more than 31,000 Cardinals fans showed up for a doubleheader to see him pitch. It was the largest crowd ever to watch a regular season game at Sportsman's Park. The turnout convinced owner Sam Breadon to insist that Dean pitch every time the team was at home for a Sunday doubleheader. Dean, who had only a seventh-grade education, was shrewd enough to know his popularity was behind the move. Throughout his career in St. Louis, Dean routinely threatened to go on strike unless his contract was renegotiated. If that failed, he would leave the team, often for days at a time.

In 1933, Dean's right arm couldn't deliver a title for St. Louis and his 20 wins didn't prevent the Cardinals from finishing in fifth place. But with the arrival of Ducky Medwick and Leo Durocher, the pieces were coming together for the Cardinals to reclaim the pennant. And when Frankie Frisch replaced Gabby Street as manager, no one benefited more than the free-spirited Dean. For him, the best was yet to come and it was right around the corner.

Burleigh Grimes
Pitcher, 1930 - 1931; 1933 - 1934

Burleigh Grimes was a spitball pitcher with a nasty disposition. He also was a five-time 20-game winner when he came to the Cardinals during the 1930 season.

Nicknamed "Old Stubblebeard" for never shaving on the days he pitched, Grimes had his greatest fame with Brooklyn, where he won 158 games in nine seasons.

He also had a well-deserved reputation for throwing at batters. Once, when the Chicago Cubs arrived in town, catcher Gabby Hartnett told the train's porter not to bother cleaning the cinders off his suit jacket, saying, "Never mind, Mr. Grimes will dust me off this afternoon."

Grimes' arrival in St. Louis at the trading deadline in 1930 seemed to breath new life into the Cardinals. With the team in fourth place, seven games out, Grimes went 13-6 and the Cardinals won 39 of their last 49 games to capture the pennant. But in the World Series, Grimes lost both his starts, despite allowing only five hits in each game.

In 1931, he won 17 games and found his revenge against the Athletics in the World Series. He threw a two-hitter to win Game 3 and was the victor in the decisive Game 7.

At the age of 40, Grimes finished his career in the majors with the New York Yankees, combative as ever. That season, while facing Detroit, Grimes gave up a home run to Tiger outfielder Goose Goslin. Later, while Goslin was standing in the on-deck circle, Grimes threw at him and knocked him to the ground. After the game, the pitcher told reporters, "He was inching up there, not content to wait his turn. So I let him have it."

Grimes later managed the Brooklyn Dodgers for two years before spending 10 seasons managing in the minor leagues. He was elected to the Hall of Fame in 1964.

Chick Hafey and Al Simmons
World Series, 1931

Two future Hall of Famers pose for cameramen before Game 1 at Sportsman's Park in St. Louis. Chick Hafey's .347 average during the regular season had earned him the National League batting title. Al Simmons had won his second consecutive American League batting crown by hitting .390 and driving in 128 runs.

The World Series featured the third straight appearance by Philadelphia and offered a rematch of the 1930 contest against St. Louis. But this time, the Cardinals, paced by Pepper Martins' hitting and base running, edged the Athletics in seven games. Simmons batted .333 with two home runs and eight RBI, while Hafey managed only four hits and batted .167.

Mr. and Mrs. Pepper Martin
1931

Following his heroic performance in the 1931 World Series, Pepper Martin became an instant celebrity. Reporters and photographers clamored to tell the story of his colorful life. Shown here with wife, Ruby, Martin was in such demand that he put team owner Sam Breadon in charge of fielding the endorsement offers that came his way. He was even booked on the vaudeville circuit so that people could see him in person and hear his stories about the series. But the simple country boy left the circuit after only a month. He said it felt like stealing to do so little for so much money. He returned to Oklahoma and spent the offseason hunting and fishing.

Pepper Martin and Ripper Collins
Spring Training, c. 1932

Pepper Martin and Ripper Collins were the heart and soul of the fabled Gas House Gang. Never shy about performing for an audience, the duo worked up pantomimes and performed before games. Martin also was famous for juggling a baseball behind his back, amazing fans with his dexterity.

Here, Martin and Collins are shown demonstrating their imaginary boating routine. The young man in the middle was adopted as a team mascot. Nicknamed "Yoyo," he suffered from Down's Syndrome and was befriended by Martin.

Joe "Ducky" Medwick
Outfielder, 1932 - 1940; 1947 - 1948

Joseph "Ducky" Medwick was the toughest guy on a team full of tough guys. He was a hard-nosed ballplayer who hit everything that came his way, baseballs and teammates alike. His chiseled physique earned him the nickname "Muscles."

The son of Hungarian immigrants, Medwick joined the Cardinals late in 1932 and quickly became a fixture in left field, taking over for the recently traded Chick Hafey.

Medwick became one of the National League's most feared hitters. A notorious bad-ball hitter, Medwick was a power hitter who also hit for a high average. Beginning in 1934, he had six straight seasons with more than 100 RBI and never hit below .319. He twice led the league in hits and in 1937, he won the league's MVP award. His slashing line drives also produced seven straight seasons with at least 40 doubles.

Like the other members of the Gas House Gang, Medwick was driven to win at all costs. He frequently fought with teammates and led by intimidation. During a game Dizzy Dean was pitching at Forbes Field in Pittsburgh, Medwick got a late jump on a fly ball down the line, allowing three runs to score. Dean left the mound and headed towards Medwick, glaring in displeasure. When the inning ended, the two exchanged words in the dugout. When the Dean brothers both started towards Medwick, Ducky grabbed a bat and offered to separate the two. The next inning, Medwick hit a grand slam to give the Cardinals back the lead. When he returned to the dugout, he took a long drink from the water fountain, walked the length of the bench and spit a stream of water on Dean's shoes, saying, "There's your three runs back and one more. Now let's see you hold the lead."

Early in the 1940 season, Medwick and pitcher Curt Davis, who won 22 games for St. Louis in 1939, were sold to the Brooklyn Dodgers for four players and $125,000. Six days later, in a game against the Cardinals, Medwick was beaned and knocked unconscious by St. Louis pitcher Bob Bowman. The two had exchanged words in a hotel elevator earlier that day. Although he continued to hit for average, Medwick's power numbers fell off dramatically. He spent the next six years with the Dodgers and Giants before returning to the Cardinals as a reserve in 1947. But at age 35, he was through in the majors. Medwick managed in the minor leagues for three seasons before returning to St. Louis and going into the insurance business. In 1966, he began serving as the Cardinals' minor-league hitting instructor. Medwick was elected to the Hall of Fame in 1968. He died in 1975.

Frankie Frisch
Manager, 1933 - 1937

When Frankie Frisch replaced Gabby Street as manager midway through 1933, he'd played seven seasons with the Cardinals and was a natural leader on the field.

Frisch's energy and hustling style proved contagious. He argued with umpires, never gave an inch and blended the Cardinals' veterans and rookies into a cohesive unit. And with Branch Rickey's farm system in place, he reaped a steady flow of young talent like Paul Dean and Johnny Mize.

Frisch also managed to handle the big personalities on the Cardinals roster. He was willing to overlook the off-field shenanigans of Pepper Martin, Leo Durocher and others so long as they played hard and delivered on the field. But he stressed that the team came first. When Dizzy and Paul Dean missed an exhibition game during the 1934 season, Frisch fined them both. The brothers threatened to go on strike unless the fines were rescinded, but Frisch stood firm and the Deans backed down. It was a defining moment in Frisch's leadership. The result was 95 wins and a championship in 1934.

In 1935, the Cardinals won 96 games, but finished second to the Chicago Cubs, who won 100. When the team finished second again in 1936 and fourth in 1937, Frisch's time at the helm was running out. With two weeks left in the 1938 season and the Cardinals in sixth place, Frisch was fired by Sam Breadon.

Frisch spent another 10 seasons managing the Pirates, then the Cubs, and was elected to the Hall of Fame in 1947. In 1973, he was seriously injured in an auto accident and died a month later at age 74.

Leo Durocher
Shortstop, 1933 - 1937

The Cardinals brought shortstop Leo Durocher to St. Louis after Charlie Gelbert hurt himself in a hunting accident. Durocher's value lay in his glove, not in his bat. He was such a poor hitter during his first five seasons in the majors that he earned the nickname, "the All-American Out."

Durocher was brash, outspoken and one of the game's most vicious bench jockeys. His constant stream of insults toward opposing players, managers and umpires earned him the wrath of the league. Durocher's antics rubbed the college-educated Frankie Frisch the wrong way, but their on-field chemistry was smooth and so Frisch tutored him at the plate to keep him in the lineup. Under Frisch, Durocher had the three best years of his career at the plate.

Off the field, Durocher was a hustler. He bet on anything that moved, frequented pool halls and race tracks, hung out with mobsters and was the sharpest dresser on the team. Traded to the Brooklyn Dodgers in 1938, his lasting fame came as a major league manager. Durocher piloted the Dodgers to the 1941 National League pennant and the New York Giants to titles in 1951 and 1954. He later managed the Chicago Cubs and Houston Astros.

Durocher was elected to the Hall of Fame in 1994, three years after his death.

France Laux
Announcer, 1929 - 1946

For almost two decades, radio announcer France Laux was the voice of the Cardinals.

From his perch at Sportsman's Park, Laux described the action for listeners at home, reaching fans in dozens of states over the powerful, 50,000-watt KMOX. When the team was on the road, he called the games from the studio using the Western Union teletype for details. And as one of radio's early pioneers, he was chosen to broadcast nine World Series and eight All-Star games.

Laux's play-by-play coverage was later criticized as too laid back. Objective almost to a fault, his monotone descriptions would stand in sharp contrast to the colorful and emotional commentators who would follow him.

In the mid-1940s, Cardinals owner Sam Breadon, tired of sharing radio time with the American League's Browns, started looking at broadcast options and Laux found himself out of baseball.

Laux spent another seven years at KMOX covering basketball, football and hockey, then retired after the 1953 season. He ran a local bowling alley for several years and even served as president of the American Bowling Congress. Laux died in 1978 at the age of 80.

Dizzy and Paul Dean
1934

By the time pitcher Paul Dean reached the majors in 1934, his brother Dizzy had told everyone that his little brother was even faster than he was.

Reporters asked Dizzy for a prediction on the 1934 season, then printed a story claiming the Dean brothers would win 45 games. The boast likely came from Branch Rickey, but took on a life of its own. Still, the Dean brothers set out to back it up.

They got off to a slow start but warmed with the weather. Dizzy's record stood at 18-3 at the end of July, but he was constantly sparring with the front office over the brothers' salaries. In August, both were fined for missing an exhibition game. Yet despite missing two starts, Paul won 19 games by season's end. Dizzy won his final seven starts to win 30 for the season. When St. Louis finally clinched the pennant, the Dean brothers had won 49 games.

The highlight came on September 21 when the Cardinals played a doubleheader in Brooklyn. Dizzy pitched the first game, a three-hit shut-out. In the second game, Paul went one better. He threw a no-hitter, allowing only one walk to the Dodger lineup.

In the World Series against the Tigers, the pair was overpowering. They each won two games, with Dizzy blanking Detroit in Game 7 to give the Cardinals the championship.

Leo Durocher and Pepper Martin
Polo Grounds, 1933

No two players typified the win-at-all-costs attitude of the Gas House Gang more than shortstop Leo Durocher and third baseman Pepper Martin. Winning was all that mattered to Durocher and he didn't care how he did it. He told reporters, "If I was playing third base and my mother was rounding third with the winning run, I'd trip her. I'd pick her up and say, "Sorry mom, but nobody beats me.' "

Durocher and Martin, who moved from the outfield to third base in 1933, gave the Cardinals a superb defensive tandem on the left side of the infield. Durocher's range ensured he got everything hit his way. Martin's strong arm allowed him to knock down balls with his chest, recover and throw the runner out at first. Despite the dangers of playing the hot corner, Martin never wore a protective cup. Durocher later recalled, "I've seen him get hit by the ball in every corner of his body, except the important one. He was just a lucky man, I guess."

Martin often played hurt, once playing an entire game with a broken finger on his throwing hand. Only after the adhesive wrapping unraveled following a throw to first did Martin's injury become known. Asked about it by reporters after the game, Martin replied, "It's only a small bone."

Like Durocher, Martin couldn't stand the thought of being beaten. When opposing batters started bunting to take advantage of his sore back, Martin would field the ball and throw it at the runner's head, dropping him before he reached first base. Word spread quickly around the league and the bunting soon stopped.

Perhaps Durocher summed up the team's tough attitude best, saying, "We fought amongst ourselves, yes, but God forbid if anybody picked a fight with us, because then they'd have to lick all 23 Cardinals."

Paul "Daffy" Dean
Pitcher, 1934 - 1939

When the Dean brothers combined for 49 wins in 1934, the sharecropper's sons from rural Arkansas became the toast of St. Louis. But their success was not to last.

When Paul Dean arrived in St. Louis as the second half of a famous-family pitching duo, it was a marketer's dream come true. While Dizzy was loud, a braggart and one of the game's greatest showmen, Paul was quiet and reserved. Content to let Dizzy do the talking, the press dubbed Paul "Harpo" after the famous Marx brother who never spoke. Later, they decided that Dizzy and Daffy sounded better together. Paul found the nickname insulting and detested it.

Paul's stock in trade was a fastball delivered with a sidearm motion that tailed away from opposing hitters. Unlike Dizzy, who mixed his heater with a devastating curveball, Paul got by on control and sheer speed.

In 1935, the brothers had another great year, with Paul winning 19 games and Dizzy winning 28. Although St. Louis finished second to the Cubs, Cardinals fans were sure the Dean brothers would lead them to a string of championships.

The next spring, Paul held out in a contract dispute. His 1934 salary had been $3,000 and he'd received only a small bump after winning 19 games in 1935. Paul sat out the entire spring, but eventually came back for a token pay raise.

In 1936, during a 12-inning complete game victory in Chicago, Paul felt a twinge in his pitching arm. The next day, he could barely lift it. He later played, but lost four games before shutting down for the season. His career in the majors was essentially over.

Paul pitched in a single game in 1937 before doctors decided to operate, ending his season. When he returned to the Cardinals in 1938, his speed was gone. So was his brother. Dizzy, who also injured his arm and had been traded to the Cubs. For his part, Paul would win just three more games over the next two seasons. In 1940, he was traded to the New York Giants. There, he was used mostly in relief. A final comeback attempt with the Browns in 1943 lasted 13 innings, but Paul Dean was through. He was 30 years old.

Dean later owned several minor league teams in Texas and New Mexico before retiring to Arkansas where he died in 1981 at age 67.

Virgil "Spud" Davis and Bill DeLancey
Spring Training, 1934

Unlike many National League teams of their era, the 1930s Cardinals never had an all-star caliber player behind the plate. The Cubs had Gabby Hartnett, the Reds had Ernie Lombardi and the Dodgers had Al Lopez, but St. Louis utilized a platoon system. In 1934, it was Davis and DeLancey.

Spud Davis spent 16 years in the majors, was a superb hitter and an excellent signal caller. He played three seasons in St. Louis before being traded to Cincinnati in 1937. He spent his final seven seasons as a backup.

DeLancey came to the Cardinals as a 32-year-old rookie in 1934 and proceeded to hit .316 with 13 home runs and 40 RBI in 80 games. Branch Rickey predicted stardom because of his strong throwing arm. But the next year, DeLancey was diagnosed with tuberculosis and sent home. He missed the next four seasons and after 15 games in 1940, he retired to the Arizona desert. He died six years later on his 45th birthday.

Dizzy Dean
World Series, 1934

Always the showman, Dizzy Dean posed for photographers before Game 2 of the 1934 World Series at Navin Field in Detroit. He and his brother Paul arrived late, having had lunch at the palatial estate of automaker Henry Ford. Already ahead 1-0 in the series, Dean was in especially high spirits. He decided to entertain the stadium's massive crowd with a rendition of "Wagon Wheels." He joined the brass band behind home plate and commandeered a tuba from a startled band member. Following his musical number, Dean chided the musician, saying, "Give me a week and I'll have your job." Dean then sauntered over to the Tigers dugout and began taunting the Detroit players, apologizing in a mock tone for his mediocre performance the day before. Dean promised he would "show you my real good stuff the next time out." He kept his promise by shutting out the Tigers in the decisive Game 7.

Back in St. Louis, record crowds lined the streets of downtown to welcome the Cardinals with a ticker-tape parade. Paul rode in the same convertible with Dizzy and his wife, Pat. Dizzy, wearing a white pith helmet, swung an inflatable tiger from a noose. The brothers immediately departed for a two-week barnstorming tour against an all-star Negro Leagues squad. They followed with a one-week vaudeville routine on Broadway before filming a Warner Brothers short entitled *Dizzy and Daffy*. The dozens of personal appearances and endorsement deals netted Dizzy over $65,000 in only 18 months. It proved a nice bonus for a player whose regular season salary was $8,500.

Frankie Frisch, Joe Medwick and Commissioner Landis
World Series, 1934

During Game 7 in Detroit, with the Cardinals ahead 9-0 after six innings, manager Frankie Frisch (far left) and his left fielder, Ducky Medwick, were summoned to the commissioner's box near the first-base dugout. In the third inning, Medwick had tripled and slid hard into Tigers third baseman Marv Owen. The two exchanged words and a shoving match broke out. Tigers fans, already upset at being behind 7-0, waited until Medwick took his position in left field the next inning and began pelting him with assorted fruit, vegetables and soda bottles. Stadium attendants had to clear the field after each inning and by the seventh, Commissioner Kennesaw Mountain Landis had seen enough. He ordered Frisch to remove Medwick from the game for his own safety. Frisch complied and St. Louis, with Dizzy Dean on the mound, went on to win, 11-0, and claim the championship.

Walter Alston
First baseman, 1936

Walter Alston built a Hall of Fame career as a major league manager. He spent 23 years with the Brooklyn — and later Los Angeles — Dodgers, where he won seven National League pennants and four World Series.

As a player, he was far less successful.

Alston began his baseball career in 1935 as a third baseman in the minor leagues. The next year, he hit .326 with 35 home runs and 114 RBI and late in the season, the Cardinals called him up. In his only at bat, Alston struck out. He played another 11 years in the minors, but never made it back to the majors as a player.

In 1940, at age 29, Alston was named player-manager in the Dodgers' minor-league chain. In 1949, he led St. Paul to the American Association title and was promoted to manage the Dodgers' top farm club in Montreal. There, he won two titles in four years.

Alston's success earned him a ticket to manage in the majors. Alston took over the Brooklyn Dodgers in 1954 and won the National League pennant in 1955 and 1956. By 1958, the team had moved to Los Angeles, where Alston won a third title the next season. In 1976, at age 64, Alston stepped down as manager of the Dodgers. He was elected to the Hall of Fame in 1983 and died the following year.

Elwin "Preacher" Roe
Pitcher, 1938

Preacher Roe was a late bloomer who became a 20-game winner at age 36.

Roe was a tall, skinny country boy from Arkansas who signed with the Cardinals for $5,000, a hunting dog and a fishing rod. Eager to get a return on their investment, St. Louis sent the 22-year-old directly to the big leagues. It proved a short stay.

In his only appearance, Roe gave up six hits and four runs in three innings. The Cardinals sent him back to the minors and five years later, sold him to the Pittsburgh Pirates for $25,000. There, in 1945, he won 15 games and led the National League in strike-outs.

But an off-season injury almost ended his career. Coaching the local high school basketball team back home in Arkansas, Roe got into a fight with a referee. The referee knocked Roe over the team bench and fractured his skull.

When he returned to baseball in the spring, his fastball—and his effectiveness—was gone. He wound up with Branch Rickey in Brooklyn and after adding a change-up to his pitching repertoire, he began to win. In 1949, he went 15-6 and was the only Dodgers pitcher to win a game against the Yankees in that fall's World Series. The next season Roe won 19 games and made the All-Star team. But his greatest season was yet to come.

In 1951, the 35-year-old Roe went 22-3. It was the highest winning percentage in the National League since 1940. He threw 19 complete games and two shut-outs. But it would be his last big year.

Roe moved to the Ozark Mountains of Missouri and opened a grocery store. After he retired, Roe and his catcher, Roy Campanella, admitted that Roe had extended his career by relying on an illegal pitch, the spitball.

Johnny Mize
First baseman, 1936 - 1941

Slugger Johnny Mize was a big bear of a man who became one of the most consistent hitters in the National League. Mize also is living proof that the best deals are sometimes those never made.

In the spring of 1935, the 22-year-old Mize was sold to the Cincinnati Reds for $55,000, contingent on him being healthy. Mize, who had batted .339 the previous year with Rochester, needed an operation to remove bone spurs in his leg. When he had trouble hitting and running that spring, the Reds cancelled the sale. Back in St. Louis, the operation was a success and Mize joined the Cardinals for good the next year. His arrival brought a major offensive boost. Mize batted .329 and hit 19 home runs while sharing first base duties

with veteran Rip Collins. Collins was soon traded to give Mize the everyday job.

In 1937, Mize blossomed into a ferocious combination of power and average. He batted .364 and his 25 home runs and 113 RBI were second on the team only to Ducky Medwick, the National League's MVP. That year began a stretch of six straight seasons where Mize drove in at least 100 RBI.

In 1938, Mize batted .337 and his 16 doubles led the league. The next year, he was even stronger. He slugged 28 home runs and 44 doubles and won the NL batting title. Not since the days of "Sunny Jim" Bottomley had Cardinals fans seen such a superb run producer at first base.

In 1940, Mize would amaze St. Louis fans with his best year yet.

Ducky Medwick, Leo Durocher, Pepper Martin, Johnny Mize
Spring Training, 1937

By 1937, the Gas House Gang was no more. The only remaining regulars from the 1934 championship team were Ducky Medwick and Pepper Martin. The Cardinals booming bats couldn't keep the team from finishing in fourth place. Despite leading the National League in doubles and stolen bases, St. Louis went 81-73 and trailed the pennant-winning Giants by 15 games.

Ducky Medwick had the greatest year of his career. His Triple Crown season was supplemented by Johnny Mize's .364 average and 113 RBI. Pepper Martin batted .304, but played in only 98 games. For his part, Leo Durocher would bat an anemic .203 and be traded to Brooklyn after the season.

The Cardinals pitching staff was partly to blame. Dizzy Dean broke his big toe at the All-Star game, then developed arm problems. He would win just 13 games in this, his last decent season. His brother Paul, winner of 38 games in his first two seasons, missed all but one game that season and was never the same. Only starter Lon Warneke won more than 15 games. It would be five long seasons before Cardinals fans would see another championship banner flying over Sportsman's Park.

Ducky Medwick's batting grip

These are the hands and wrists that produced one of the greatest offensive seasons ever by a St. Louis Cardinals hitter. In 1937, Ducky Medwick led the National League in every offensive category except triples. He batted .374, hit 31 home runs and drove in 154 runs to win the Triple Crown, the only Cardinal besides Rogers Hornsby to do so. Medwick's 237 hits remain the second highest single-season total in club history and his 154 RBI remain the Cardinals' all-time single-season record.

Lon Warneke
Pitcher, 1937 - 1942

Lon Warneke first signed with the Cardinals, but his best years came with the Chicago Cubs.

Warneke joined the Cardinals' farm team in 1928 at age 19, but he was released after winning only six games. The next year, he won 16 games for another club and the Cubs picked him up for $10,000. He quickly made it to Chicago and in 1932, he won 22 games, helping the Cubs claim the National League pennant. Soon he became the workhorse of the Cubs' pitching staff, leading the team in innings pitched for four straight years. In 1933, his 26 complete games led the league.

Warneke had a sizzling fastball and a reputation as an excellent fielder. He was a three-time 20-game winner for Chicago, and in five full seasons, he won 98 games. In the 1935 World Series against Detroit, he was the only Cubs pitcher to defeat the Tigers. The next year, he won 16 games and his four shut-outs led the league.

Warneke was traded to the Cardinals in 1937 for first baseman Ripper Collins and pitcher Roy Parmelee. It was a steal for St. Louis. Collins had lost his first-base job to rookie Johnny Mize and Parmelee had won 11 games in his only season with the Cardinals. Warneke paid immediate dividends, winning 18 games his first year. A local sportswriter dubbed him the "Arkansas Hummingbird" for his speed and pinpoint control. Warneke went 77-48 in five full seasons with St. Louis. In 1941, he threw the season's only no-hitter against the defending champion Cincinnati Reds. Early in the 1942 season, the Cubs were so desperate to get him back that they paid the Cardinals $75,000. But at age 33, his arm was shot. He went 10-13 in parts of three seasons with Chicago.

To stay close to the game, Warneke went behind the plate and began a second career as an umpire. After three seasons of calling balls and strikes in the Pacific Coast League, he returned to the National League in 1949 for seven seasons. He remains the only major-leaguer to play and umpire in both the All-Star game and the World Series. In 1955, he returned to his farm in Arkansas and in 1962, he was elected a civil court judge in Garland County, a position he held for 10 years. He died of a heart attack in 1976.

Enos "County" Slaughter
Outfielder, 1938 - 1942; 1946 - 1953

Enos Slaughter's hustle made him a fan favorite and a fixture in St. Louis for more than a decade.

At a time when the Cardinals' farm system included dozens of teams and hundreds of players, Slaughter's meteoric rise to the majors was unheard of. His third season in the minors, he led the American Association with 245 hits and a .382 average. The next spring, he was installed as the Cardinals' everyday right fielder.

Slaughter possessed an exceptionally strong throwing arm and base runners learned not to challenge his deadly accuracy. Slaughter also was a gifted hitter. In 1939, he led the National League with 52 doubles and batted .320. And when the Cardinals won the NL pennant in 1942, Slaughter led the league with 188 hits and 17 triples.

After three years in the service during World War II, Slaughter returned to the Cardinals in 1946. The layoff had little effect as he promptly led the league with 130 RBI. And in that fall's World Series against the Boston Red Sox, his aggressive base running in Game 7 won the title for St. Louis.

With the game tied 3-3, Slaughter singled to lead off the eighth inning. On a long single by Harry Walker into the outfield gap, Slaughter ran through the stop sign thrown up by the Cardinals' third base coach and shocked everyone in the ballpark by scoring the winning run. Nicknamed the "Mad Dash," Slaughter's daring gamble paid off and is still talked about almost 60 years later.

Over the next seven years, Slaughter was a consistent run producer for St. Louis. In 1949, he again led the league in triples and twice drove in more than 100 runs in a season. But after three straight second-place finishes, the St. Louis franchise was entering a period of sustained decline. Despite the slugging of Slaughter and teammate Stan Musial, the Cardinals were rarely a serious pennant contender during the 1950s. The 1946 pennant would be the team's last for 18 years.

For his part, Slaughter played in another three World Series, none of them in a Cardinals uniform.

The Mudcat Band
New York City, 1938

Pepper Martin formed a musical group among his teammates during the glory days of the Gas House Gang. Although the lineup changed over the years, Martin remained the one constant. The group entertained on lengthy train trips, in hotel lobbies and anywhere they could astound an audience with their musical mayhem. Patterned after the jug bands of the rural South, the group wore custom-made cowboy outfits emblazoned with the Cardinals' team logo. They roared through versions of "Buffalo Gals," "Possum Up a Gum Stump" and the ever popular, "Willie, My Toes Are Cold." Talent was never a prerequisite for membership.

Shown above are (seated from left) pitcher Max Lanier on guitar and maestro Pepper Martin on guitar. Standing (starting from the left) are pitcher Bob Weiland on jug, pitcher Bill McGee on fiddle and reserve Stanley "Frenchy" Bordagaray on washboard.

Jimmy Brown
Infielder, 1937 - 1943

Jimmy Brown was a scrappy reserve infielder who shuffled between positions because of his weak arm.

Brown joined the Cardinals after four seasons in the minors where he had become a switch-hitter. He was small, but hit for average and rarely struck out. And his fiery attitude made him one of Branch Rickey's favorites. During a game the Cardinals were losing badly, a reserve player criticized a teammate for making an error. Brown warned the critic, "Don't be second-guessing guys on this ball club." Then he punched the guy in the face.

Brown's only season as the Cardinals' shortstop in 1939 ended with the arrival of rookie Marty Marion in 1940. Shuffled back and forth between second and third base, Brown was the Cardinals' primary lead-off hitter and twice he led the National League in at-bats. In 1942, he drove in a career high 71 RBI and batted .300 in the World Series against the Yankees. Brown spent two-plus seasons in the military during World War II. When he returned in 1946, he played one season with Pittsburgh before returning to the minors as a manager. Brown served as a coach with the Boston Braves for three years before managing in the minors for another decade.

Howie Krist
Pitcher, 1937 - 1938; 1941 - 1943; 1946

Right-hander Howie Krist's promising career was constantly interrupted by injuries and later, service in World War II. After Krist won 20 games in the South Atlantic League, he joined the Cardinals late in 1937. Used primarily as a reliever, he went 3-1. The next season, he suffered a severe case of influenza, missed spring training and was returned to the minors. There, with Rochester in 1938, he fractured his ankle. In 1939, he underwent an operation to remove bone chips from his elbow. Finally healthy, he won 22 games for Houston in 1940.

In 1941, Krist was a perfect 10-0 with the Cardinals. When St. Louis won the 1942 pennant, he was the team's most effective reliever, going 13-3. In 1943, Krist split time between the bullpen and the starting rotation, going 11-5 and throwing three shut-outs. But World War II intervened and Krist joined an infantry division in France, where he suffered leg wounds. By the time he returned in 1946, he was no longer in shape to pitch. Arm problems got him shipped back to the minors and he retired after a single season. Krist returned to western New York state and operated a furniture store for the next 30 years.

Curt Davis
Pitcher, 1938 - 1940

Curt Davis, a superb pitcher who pitched for bad teams, came to the Cardinals from the Chicago Cubs in the trade for Dizzy Dean. A three-time All-Star, Davis was a sinkerball pitcher who forced batters to beat the ball into the ground.

Despite twice winning 20 games in the Pacific Coast League for the San Francisco Seals, Davis didn't make it to the major leagues until the age of 30, and then he played for the lowly Phillies. Davis won 19 games as a rookie, but was traded to the Cubs in 1936 and after a sore arm limited him to 10 victories in 1937, he was traded to the Cardinals the next year.

His first season in St. Louis, Davis went 12-8 and threw a one-hitter against the Brooklyn Dodgers. Davis also was an excellent hitter. He had 11 career home runs, including a grand slam for the Cardinals in 1938.

In 1939, Davis had the best year of his career, winning 22 games. But when he developed arm problems and started 0-4 in 1940, he and veteran Ducky Medwick were traded to the Dodgers for four players and $125,000 in cash.

With Brooklyn, Davis went 66-54 in five-plus seasons. Davis then spent two years in the minors before retiring after the 1947 season.

Don Padgett
Outfielder, Catcher; 1937 - 1941

Don Padgett's best year with the Cardinals was his first. As a rookie outfielder in 1937, he batted .314, hit 10 home runs and drove in 74 runs.

But the Cardinals needed more offense behind the plate and tried to convert Padgett to a catcher. Over the Christmas holidays, Padgett received a large box at home. Inside, he found a set of catchers' gear and four catchers' mitts. The present was Branch Rickey's way of telling Padgett that his future was behind the plate.

The next spring, Padgett was tutored on the fine points of handling a pitching staff and calling a game, but the results were mixed at best. Padgett had trouble handling pop-up fouls and never mastered the art of shifting his body to block low pitches in the dirt. In 1938, he split time behind the plate with Mickey Owen, who batted .271. Over the next two seasons, he caught less than half the Cardinals' games, and by 1941, the experiment was over.

However, the arrival of Enos Slaughter and Terry Moore didn't leave much room in the outfield and so the Cardinals sold Padgett to the Brooklyn Dodgers after the 1941 season.

The next spring, Padgett was drafted into the Navy and spent four years in the Pacific. He returned to Brooklyn in 1946, but had put on 30 pounds and never again was an everyday player. He played two seasons with the Phillies before returning to the minor leagues at the age of 37. After two final years in the Pacific Coast League, Padgett retired to his home in North Carolina.

Ducky Medwick and Branch Rickey
Spring Training, 1939

General Manager Branch Rickey had a well-deserved reputation as a tough negotiator. Rickey used his fiery oratory and sizeable vocabulary to wear down even the most stubborn player.

Long before the days of agents, players' contracts were revisited every spring. With the ball club holding the leverage, players either accepted the terms or went home. Only the game's best players dared hold out for a better salary.

In 1937, Ducky Medwick batted .374 and won the National League's Triple Crown. His salary was $18,000. His efforts got him a raise to $20,000 for 1938. But when his batting average fell to .322 that season, Rickey cut his salary by $2,000. Medwick came to camp in Florida determined to restore his pay cut. A week of meetings with Rickey went nowhere and when Medwick left camp and returned to St. Louis, the Cardinals issued him an ultimatum: either accept the $18,000 or the Cardinals would do without him. Medwick finally returned to Florida and reluctantly accepted the team's offer for 1939. Early the next season, the Cardinals sold Medwick to the Brooklyn Dodgers for $125,000 and four players.

Years later it was revealed that Rickey's own contract called for an annual salary of $60,000 and included a special clause. Rickey received a percentage of every transaction he orchestrated for St. Louis. It was clearly a conflict of interest that helped make Rickey a very wealthy man.

Johnny Mize
1940

Cardinals slugger Johnny Mize hit his peak in 1940, belting 43 home runs, a franchise record that stood for 58 years until Mark McGwire hit 70 in 1998.

Mize also drove in a league-high 137 RBI, the most by a Cardinal until McGwire's 147 in 1998.

Mize came back strong the next year, too, batting .317 and leading the National League with 39 doubles. But his modest 16 home runs in 1941 convinced the St. Louis front office that his power had waned and so the Cardinals traded the 28-year-old Mize to the New York Giants for three mediocre players and $50,000. It was a lousy deal for St. Louis.

Mize spent the 1942 season with New York and then joined the Navy for three years during World War II. When he returned in 1946, he quickly regained his old form. In 1947, he led the league with 51 home runs and 138 RBI. And in 1948, his 40 homers were again tops in the league.

Traded to the Yankees in 1950, Mize moved to a backup role as the club's primary pinch-hitter. He played in five straight World Series with the Yankees and in the 1952 classic, hit three home runs.

Mize retired after the 1953 season with 359 home runs and a career .312 batting average. He was elected to the Hall of Fame in 1980.

Terry Moore
Outfielder, 1935 - 1942; 1946 - 1948

Terry Moore's ability to run down fly balls and throw out base runners made him a favorite of Cardinals fans for more than a decade. With Stan Musial and Enos Slaughter, he rounded out what was universally recognized as the National League's best outfield of the era.

Moore began his career playing semi-pro ball around St. Louis, where he helped support his divorced mother. The Cardinals signed him in 1932 and sent the 20-year-old to the minor leagues, but Moore sat out the next season because he needed to make more money. Branch Rickey convinced him to stay with the game and after batting .328 for Columbus in 1934, Moore made the move to the majors the next season.

Moore quickly established his reputation at the plate and in the field. Late in 1936, he went six for six against the Boston Braves. In 1936 and 1940, he led the league's outfielders in put-outs. In 1939, he set a major-league record for outfielders by making only two errors in a season. In 1942, he put together a 20-game hitting streak. And in the World Series against the Yankees, Moore's running catch of a drive by Joe DiMaggio preserved a 2-0 Cardinals victory in Game 3.

He was selected to four consecutive All-Star teams starting in 1939.

Moore was a quiet and classy individual, whose career was often overshadowed by his more colorful teammates. Still, his fearless defensive style sometimes threatened his career. In 1938, he crashed into the outfield wall and missed two months of the season. And in 1941, a bean ball gave him a concussion and left him dizzy for months.

Like many of the Cardinals' veteran players, Moore missed several years due to military service. When he returned in 1946, he was 34 and would be an everyday player in only one of the three remaining years he spent with St. Louis.

Moore turned down an offer to manage the team in 1946, but after his retirement in 1948, he became a coach with the Cardinals for four seasons. In 1954, he briefly took over as manager of the Philadelphia Phillies, but he was replaced after the season ended. In 1956, Moore returned to coach with St. Louis for another three years.

The patch on Moore's left sleeve was worn by all major leaguers for one year (1942) to help publicize the government's health programs.

Mort Cooper
Pitcher, 1938 - 1945

Mort Cooper was a three-time 20-game winner and the National League's Most Valuable Player in 1942. His best seasons coincided with the Cardinals' three consecutive NL pennants during the war years.

Cooper also was a superstitious lot. During his first 10 years as a professional, he never won more than 13 games a year, so he tried changing his luck by switching to uniform number 13. He considered it his lucky number. Both his wife's and his son's birthdays fell on the thirteenth and his car's license plate was 1300. In 1942, after Cooper won his 13th game in July, he started a new gimmick. He wore jersey number 14 until he won his 14th, then consecutively borrowed higher numbered jerseys from his teammates until he went 22-7 and the Cardinals won their first pennant in eight years. Cooper's 10 shut-outs and 1.78 ERA led the league. Over the next two years, he went a combined 43-15.

Cooper made success a family affair. His older brother, Walker, was his catcher for his three best seasons. As they were about to play Game 2 of the 1943 World Series, the brothers learned that they'd lost their father that morning. Mort and Walker decided to "win one for Pop" and teamed up to defeat the Yankees, 4-3, for the lone Cardinals victory of the series.

In 1945, after his third straight 20-win season, Cooper asked that his salary be raised from $12,000 to $15,000. The Cardinals offered $13,500, claiming the war-time wage restrictions tied the club's hands. The Cooper brothers went on strike, with Mort leaving the team during an eastern road-trip in May. A week later, he was traded to the Boston Braves for pitcher Red Barrett and $60,000.

With Boston, Cooper won his first seven starts before elbow surgery ended his season. He returned to win 13 games in 1946, but his career in the majors was essentially over. Cooper went 3-10 in 1947 before retiring. A comeback attempt with the Cubs in 1949 lasted less than an inning. Cooper died in 1958 of cirrhosis of the liver. He was 45.

Johnny Beazley
Pitcher, 1941 - 1942; 1946

Johnny Beazley's major-league career was cut short by an arm injury, but for one season, he was the talk of the National League.

Beazley joined the Cardinals late in 1941 after winning 16 games for New Orleans. With St. Louis, he won his only start — by throwing a complete game against the Cubs. Armed with a devastating curveball and a daring change-up, Beazley was a control pitcher who stunned opposing hitters by going 21-6 his first full season. In the World Series, he twice defeated the Yankees by identical 4-3 scores.

But induction into the Army cost Beazley the next three seasons and ultimately his career. In 1944, just prior to shipping out for the Pacific, Beazley pitched a game on the West Coast against a service team led by ex-major-league catcher Harry Danning. Beazley had not been pitching and was out of shape. He threw all nine innings, but during the game, he felt something snap in his throwing shoulder. When he rejoined the Cardinals in 1946, he struggled to win seven games. He was traded to the Boston Braves in 1947, where he underwent shoulder surgery, but it was too late. He went 2-1 for Boston in three seasons before attempting several comebacks in the minor leagues.

Beazley returned to his home in Nashville, where he ran a beer distributorship and served on the city council in the 1970s.

Billy Southworth
Manager, 1940 - 1945

After 13 seasons as a major-league outfielder and 11 seasons as a minor-league manager, Billy Southworth returned to St. Louis to manage the Cardinals midway through the 1940 season.

Southworth had briefly managed the Cardinals in 1929, but his aggressive style led to his departure. After a decade of watching him school young players in the minors, Branch Rickey was convinced that Southworth had mellowed enough to merit a second chance.

When he took over for Ray Blades, the team was stuck in sixth place. But by season's end, he had driven the Cardinals to a third-place finish. The next year, the team won 97 games, its best showing in a decade.

The war-time shortage of talent actually worked to the Cardinals' advantage, with Rickey's massive farm system ensuring a steady supply of young talent. In

1942, Southworth molded a group of rookies and veterans into a team that captured the National League pennant. It was the first of three straight 100-win seasons.

Southworth was named Manager of the Year by *The Sporting News* in 1941 and 1942, and his clubs captured World Series titles in 1942 and 1944.

But a second-place finish, combined with a lavish $50,000 contract offer from the Boston Braves, persuaded Southworth to leave St. Louis after the 1945 season. In Boston, "Billy the Kid" led the formerly hapless Braves to their first title in 34 years in 1948. However, the magic was short-lived. After managing Boston to consecutive fourth-place finishes, Southworth was replaced midway through the 1951 season. He returned to his home in Ohio and died in 1969 at the age of 76.

Marty "Slats" Marion
Shortstop, 1940 - 1950
Manager, 1951

Before Ozzie Smith arrived in 1982, Marty Marion was the greatest shortstop in Cardinals history.

Marion had the three essential ingredients of a premier defensive shortstop: sure hands, great range and a strong accurate throwing arm. Despite playing in an era dominated by shortstop greats like Lou Boudreau, Pee Wee Reese and Phil Rizzuto, Marion was a seven-time All Star. The site of his lanky frame flagging down ground balls caused Pirates Manager Frankie Frisch to nickname him "the Octopus."

The Cardinals landed Marion almost by accident. In 1935, the young Marion traveled to Chattanooga where his brother, John, was playing for the Washington Senators' top minor-league club. He was given a tryout and signed to a contract. A short while later, Mary, his girlfriend and future wife, came to visit and Marion asked the club for a complimentary pass. Turned down flat, Marion demanded his release.

Later that year, Marion was persuaded to attend a Cardinals' tryout camp with his friend, Johnny Echols. Echols was offered a contract, but refused to sign unless Marion was offered one, too. The Cardinals brought both players to St. Louis so that Branch Rickey could get a closer look. Rickey signed them both and sent them to the minors. Four years later, Rickey tried to trade Marion to the Chicago Cubs, but Chicago wanted a different shortstop. Marion stayed with St. Louis and the next spring, became the Cardinals' everyday shortstop.

With Marion anchoring the St. Louis infield, the Cardinals won three straight National League pennants. In 1944, he was named the league's Most Valuable Player — the first shortstop in the history of the league to win the award. It is a tribute to his glove work that Marion won the award despite hitting just .267.

During his 11 seasons with the Cardinals, Marion led the league in put-outs twice and fielding percentage four times. But a nagging back injury shortened his career. In 1951, the 34-year-old Marion was named manager of the Cardinals, inheriting a team that finished fifth the year before. Despite leading the team to a third-place finish, he lasted only one season.

In 1952, Marion was signed to play for the St. Louis Browns, then became manager when Rogers Hornsby was fired in June. But the Browns were dreadful and Marion was fired after one season. In 1954, he was named manager of the Chicago White Sox, but Chicago couldn't compete with the American League's two most dominant teams, the Yankees and the Indians. Under Marion, the White Sox finished third twice. Forever a Cardinal, Marion spent the next 18 years running the Stadium Club for the team.

Stan Musial
September 1941

All but forgotten in baseball lore is the fact that Stan Musial was on his way to becoming a superb pitcher when an injury in the minor leagues forced him into the outfield.

In 1940, Musial was 19 and pitching for Daytona Beach in the Class D Florida State League. He was the league's top lefthander that season, going 18-5 with an ERA of 2.62. But because lower minor-league teams had small rosters, pitchers had to play the outfield on days they didn't pitch. On August 11, in the second game of a double-header against Orlando, Musial was playing centerfield when a batter hit a low line-drive into the gap. Musial dove to catch the ball backhanded, but his spikes caught in the outfield turf, slamming his left shoulder to the ground. His pitching career was through and Musial feared his path to the majors was gone, too. With a young wife and a newborn son, his monthly salary of $100 hadn't gone far and his financial situation looked bleak.

The next spring, Musial reported early to training camp in Florida, but the Cardinals considered him damaged goods. He had to beg instructors for another look. His performance in the batting cage convinced them that he might have a future as an outfielder. When camp broke, he was sent to the Cardinals' Class C team in Springfield, Missouri. There, he played every day and was free to concentrate on his hitting. The results were staggering. Musial hit .379 and drove in 94 runs in his first 87 games. He also took advantage of the ballpark's short right-field fence to hit 26 home runs, tops in the league. In late July, he was promoted to the Cardinals' top farm club in Rochester. He played in the final 54 games of the International League season and batted .326.

When the season ended, Musial returned home to Donora, Pennsylvania, to be with his young family and begin the off-season. Instead, a telegram arrived telling him to report to St. Louis for the final 12 games of the 1941 season. On September 17, Musial joined the team at Sportsman's Park. He was given a home jersey with the number six on the back and installed in right field for the injured Enos Slaughter. The Cardinals were chasing the Brooklyn Dodgers for the National League pennant and trailed by two games.

In his debut against the Boston Braves, Musial had two hits, including a two-run double in the Cardinals' victory. By season's end, the 20-year-old rookie had collected 20 hits in 12 games, including 7 RBI. The Cardinals finished in second place, but Musial's .426 average ensured that he would be given a long look the next spring.

Dizzy Dean
Broadcaster, 1941 - 1946

When arm troubles ended his major-league career, Dizzy Dean took his flamboyant personality to the radio booth.

Midway through the 1941 season, Dean left the Chicago Cubs to start a new career calling Cardinals and Browns games on the radio in St. Louis. The Griesedieck Brothers Brewing Company sponsored the games and wanted Dean as their pitchman. His job was to entertain listeners with his colorful stories and to sell beer for the brewery.

In those days, radio broadcasts of major league games were a money-losing proposition. Two tiny AM stations, WEW and WTMV in East St. Louis, owned the rights to the games, but only aired home games because of the cost of travel and long-distance phone lines. WEW carried the afternoon games and WTMV ran the night games.

Dean first took the WTMV microphone when the Yankees came to play the Browns and New York outfielder Joe DiMaggio was deep into his historic 56-game hitting streak. Soon, everyone knew Dizzy Dean was back in St. Louis.

Soon, too, came the uproar about his mangled use of the English language. "He slud into second." "He throwed him out." Dean's down-home speech delighted fans in the network's rural areas, but enraged purists. Dean took the criticism in stride. The more they complained, the higher his ratings grew and the better the brewery liked it. In 1944, his surging popularity led *The Sporting News* to name Dean their Sportscaster of the Year.

In 1947, the Cardinals decided they no longer wanted to share time with the hapless Browns, and Harry Caray and Gabby Street were chosen to call the games. Dean called the Browns games for the next three years over KWK, but left after the 1949 season.

In 1953, ABC began its weekly broadcast of the Saturday "Game of the Week" with Dean behind the microphone. For the next 12 years, his off-key rendition of "The Wabash Cannonball" made his telecasts must-see TV.

Ray Sanders
First baseman, 1942 - 1945

Ray Sanders, a product of St. Louis-area sandlots, had his best major league seasons during the war years.

In 1940, while playing for Columbus, Sanders was chosen Rookie of the Year in the American Association where he hit .308 and drove in 120 runs. The Cardinals were so impressed that they traded veteran Johnny Mize to the New York Giants to make room for the 25-year-old rookie.

The move proved shortsighted.

In the majors, Sanders was never able to reproduce Mize's power numbers. His best season came in 1944, when he batted .295 with 12 home runs and 102 RBI. The highlight of his stay in St. Louis was hitting a home run in both the 1943 and 1944 World Series.

After the 1945 season, the Cardinals decided they wanted to move Stan Musial to first base and so traded Sanders to the Boston Braves. The next August, in a game against the Cardinals at Sportsman's Park, Sanders broke his throwing arm. He underwent two operations, missed almost two full seasons and was never the same again. He played in nine games for the 1949 Braves before retiring. In 1983, Sanders was killed in an auto accident at age 66.

Max Lanier
Pitcher, 1938 - 1946; 1949 - 1951

Lefthander Max Lanier was a consistent winner for the Cardinals who gained notoriety for jumping to the Mexican League in 1946.

Lanier's three greatest seasons coincided with the Cardinals' three National League pennants between 1942 and 1944. In 1943, he went 15-7 and his 1.90 ERA was the second lowest in the league. The next year, he won 17 games and threw five shut-outs.

Like many of his fellow Cardinals, Lanier's career was interrupted by military service. He made only four appearances in 1945. But when he returned in 1946, he won his first six starts, each a complete game. Upset over his contract, Lanier staged a brief holdout before getting an extra $500, raising his annual salary to $11,000.

Meanwhile, the president of the Mexican League, a wealthy businessman named Jorge Pasquel, began offering huge contracts to lure prominent major league players south of the border. Lanier was offered a five-year contract for $14,000 a year and a reported $25,000 signing bonus. Lanier was 30 and knew he had only a few good years left. Financial security for his family played a big factor in his decision to accept Pasquel's offer.

Major league owners were outraged by the outlaw league's tactics and the Commissioner quickly ruled that any player who went to Mexico would face a five-year suspension from the major leagues. Many of the game's biggest stars, including the Cardinals' own Stan Musial, were approached with offers, but few accepted.

Lanier found playing conditions in Mexico were a far cry from the major leagues. Word of long bus rides, run-down stadiums and lousy accommodations filtered back to the States and kept many other veterans from following him. In addition, a player revolt by Hispanic players and mounting financial losses by the Mexican League's eight teams forced Pasquel to make changes. By the second season, he began cutting player salaries and the dozen or so American players began returning home. Facing suspension, Lanier and others sued Major League Baseball to get their jobs back. In 1949, baseball agreed to reinstate Lanier and the others.

Lanier went a combined 27-22 in three seasons for St. Louis before being traded to the Giants in 1952. He retired the next year and managed briefly in the minor leagues. His son, Hal, also played and managed in the majors.

Harry "The Hat" Walker
Outfielder, 1940 - 1943; 1946 - 1947; 1950 - 1951; 1955
Manager, 1955

Harry Walker spent almost two decades playing and managing in the major leagues.

He became the everyday outfielder with the Cardinals in 1943 after six years in the minors and batted .294 his first season. At the plate, he had a habit of removing and adjusting his cap between every pitch, earning him the nickname "the Hat."

Two years of military service in Europe during World War II interrupted his playing career. He served in the Army under General George Patton and was awarded the Purple Heart and a Bronze Star. He returned to the Cardinals in 1946 and in that fall's World Series against the Boston Red Sox, batted .412, led the Cardinals with six RBI and drove in the game-winning run in Game 7 to give St. Louis the championship.

Only 10 games into the 1947 season, Walker was traded to the Phillies. It was a move St. Louis would soon regret. When his equipment was shipped to Boston, Walker was forced to borrow a heavier bat from ex-teammate Johnny Mize. He began choking up on the handle and went on to hit .363 and win the National League batting title. Coming on the heels of his brother Dixie's batting title in 1944, it marked the first time a pair of brothers had won batting titles. It also was the first time a player had won a batting title while playing for two different teams in the same season.

Walker couldn't duplicate his 1947 performance and spent the next two seasons with two different teams before re-joining the Cardinals in 1950. At age 31, he was no longer an everyday player and soon, he began managing in the Cardinals' minor-league system. In 1955, Walker took over for the departed Eddie Stanky as manager of the Cardinals for a single season. Over the next 20 years, he managed the Pirates and the Astros, in addition to several stops around the minor leagues. In 1979, he returned to his native Alabama and began coaching at the University of Alabama-Birmingham.

Stan Musial
1942

Stan Musial's meteoric climb from Class C to the major leagues didn't guarantee that the 21-year-old was in the big leagues to stay. At spring training in 1942, Musial had to crack an outfield that included veterans Terry Moore and Enos Slaughter.

Musial got off to a slow start in the Cardinals' exhibition games and was benched by manager Billy Southworth. To rebuild his confidence, the wily Southworth batted the struggling Musial exclusively against right-handed pitchers until he found his stroke. On the train trip north, Southworth took Musial aside and assured the rookie that he was the Cardinals' starting leftfielder. Not long after, Branch Rickey tore up Musial's contract of $400 a month and gave him a raise to the princely sum of $700 a month.

In his first full season, Musial hit a respectable .315. He slowly learned the tendencies of opposing pitchers, began driving the ball to all fields and developed a reputation for clutch hitting. In 1943, Musial had the first great season of his illustrious career. He won the batting title with a lofty .357 average and his 220 hits, 48 doubles and 20 triples were all tops in the National League. For his efforts, Musial was named the league's Most Valuable Player. The following season, he again led the league in hits and doubles. His .347 average was second only to Dixie Walker's .357.

But baseball would temporarily take a back seat to world affairs. With World War II raging on, Musial would soon follow his teammates into the military.

George "Whitey" Kurowski
Third baseman, 1941 - 1949

Whitey Kurowski overcame a childhood injury to become the hero of the 1942 World Series.

When he was nine, Kurowski fell off a fence and landed on some broken glass, severely cutting his right wrist. The arm became infected and doctors wound up removing four inches of bone. Undeterred, Kurowski went on to play American Legion ball until he was discovered by a Cardinals scout. Four years later, toward the end of the 1941 season, he was promoted to the majors. The next year, installed at third base, Kurowski batted .254 and helped the Cardinals win their first pennant since 1934.

In the 1942 World Series against the heavily favored Yankees, Kurowski's clutch hitting made the difference. The Yankees won Game 1, but St. Louis came back to win the next three. In Game 5, with the score tied 2-2 in the eighth inning, Kurowski hit a two-run homer to give the Cardinals the game and the series.

Over the next five seasons, Kurowski was among the most dependable third basemen in the National League. A four-time All-Star, he hit 20 or more home runs three times, including a career-high 27 in 1947. That same season, Kurowski batted .307 and drove in a team-high 104 runs.

But bone chips in his elbow prematurely ended Kurowski's career two years later at age 31. He later managed in the minors for several years.

Branch Rickey
c. 1943

By the end of the 1941 season, Cardinals General Manager Branch Rickey was barely speaking to owner Sam Breadon.

Rickey was a brilliant innovator whose eye for talent had built an unmatched farm system and brought a string of titles to St. Louis. In a time of record profits, Rickey saw Breadon as a penny pincher.

Breadon was a businessman who grew weary of Rickey's huge salary and press coverage giving him sole credit for the team's success. When Rickey's three-year deal ended after the 1941 season, the two parted company.

Rickey accepted an offer to run the Brooklyn Dodgers, but before making the leap, he insisted on a clause in his contract allowing him to purchase 25 percent of the club's stock.

In Brooklyn, Rickey worked his magic through shrewd trades and enhanced scouting. But his success was sidetracked for three seasons as increasing numbers of players left for the war. Only by the late 1940s did Rickey's rebuilding program begin to pay dividends for the Dodgers.

The event that has become Rickey's greatest legacy happened in 1945, when he signed Jackie Robinson to the Dodgers' chain. Two years later, Robinson became the first African-American to play in the major leagues. Rickey went on to sign other black players, such as Roy Campanella and Joe Black, whose talents gave the Dodgers a leg up on the other seven NL teams. By the time Rickey left Brooklyn after eight years, his strategy had delivered two National League pennants and laid a foundation for the Dodgers' dominance in the 1950s. The pool of talent he assembled won four NL titles between 1952 and 1956. And when he left, Rickey sold his stock holdings in the Dodgers for a reported $1 million.

In 1950, Rickey migrated to Pittsburgh, where his reputation as a turn-around artist faced its toughest test. He inherited a franchise that hadn't won a pennant since 1927 and it took time for his changes to produce results. His greatest coup was drafting a young outfielder named Roberto Clemente out of the Dodgers' system in 1954. When Rickey's five-year contract was up in 1955, he left Pittsburgh. Five years later, the Pirates won the 1960 World Series.

Rickey died in 1965. He was elected to the Hall of Fame in 1967.

Marty Marion and "Red" Barrett
1945

Even the combined efforts of the Cardinals' two brightest stars couldn't bring a fourth consecutive pennant home to St. Louis in 1945.

Shortstop Marty Marion was the National League's MVP in 1944 and the team's acknowledged leader on the field. But the offense struggled the next year because the Cardinals' entire outfield — Enos Slaughter, Terry Moore and Stan Musial — were all in the service.

The burden for success fell to the pitchers.

Charles "Red" Barrett came to St. Louis early in 1945 after spending parts of six seasons with the Reds and Braves. A control pitcher who rarely walked batters, he was quick and efficient on the mound. In 1944 with the Braves, he threw a complete game victory with only 58 pitches — an all-time record.

With the Cardinals, Barrett, who had been a 20-game winner three times in the minor leagues, proceeded to have the best year of his career. He won 21 games, led the league in complete games and innings pitched, and kept the Cardinals in the race to the end. Despite winning 95 games, the Cardinals finished three games behind the Cubs.

Barrett's success was short-lived. The next season, he fell out of favor with new Cardinals manager Eddie Dyer and spent most of his season on the bench. Perhaps it was all the time that Barrett spent in nightclubs. An accomplished jazz singer, he was on a first-name basis with Tommy Dorsey and Sammy Kaye and often joined the era's best big bands on stage. After going 3-2 in 1946, Barrett was traded back to Boston. Three years later, he retired.

Stan Musial
1945

Like many of the game's biggest stars, Stan Musial's major-league career was interrupted by World War II. But unlike Ted Williams, Bob Feller and Hank Greenberg, who all missed three full seasons, Musial's military service was limited to one year.

With a wife and young son, Musial's draft board in Donora, Pennsylvania, elected not to draft him until after the 1944 season. When the call came, Musial joined the Navy and eventually was assigned to Pearl Harbor, Hawaii. Like many major-league stars, Musial was made a physical fitness instructor and played on the base's all-service team. Many military commanders stocked their outfits with former big leaguers under the guise of building morale among the troops. In reality, they wanted bragging rights in the weekly games against other bases.

Following an emergency visit home to visit his ailing father, Musial was re-assigned to the Philadelphia Naval Ship Yard and discharged two months later. With a fellow sailor, he hitchhiked home to Donora, where he spent a week with his family before leaving for spring training in Florida.

In camp, Musial faced a new position. St. Louis had traded first baseman Ray Sanders to the Boston Braves and decided to make Musial his replacement. The move and time off had little effect on Musial's performance. In 1946, he won his second batting crown with a .365 average. He also led the National League in hits, doubles, triples and runs scored. St. Louis captured its fourth pennant in five years, then defeated the Boston Red Sox in the World Series. "Stan the Man" was back and all seemed right in Cardinals land.

Harry " The Cat" Brecheen
Pitcher, 1940; 1943 - 1952

Harry Brecheen was the pitching hero of the Cardinals' 1946 World Series victory.

Brecheen was used in relief when he joined the Cardinals pitching staff for good in 1943, but he quickly moved into the starting rotation. In 1944, he won 16 games and threw a complete-game victory in Game 4 of the World Series against the Browns, the only all-St. Louis World Series ever held.

In 1945, he went 14-4 and his 2.52 ERA was the lowest on the pitching staff. The next year, he was a mediocre 15-15, although he threw five shut-outs. But in the World Series against the Boston Red Sox, he was dazzling.

After Boston won the opening game, Brecheen responded with a four-hit shut-out in Game 2 to even the series. When the Red Sox won Games 3 and 5, the Cardinals suddenly faced elimination. In Game 6, Brecheen scattered eight hits and with the help of three double-plays, won the game 4-1. In Game 7, with St. Louis holding a 3-1 lead after seven innings, Brecheen was summoned to relieve Cardinals starter Murry Dickson with two runners on base. Both runners scored, tying the game 3-3, but Brecheen became the game's winning pitcher when St. Louis rallied behind Enos Slaughter's dramatic dash around the bases in the bottom of the eighth. Brecheen became the first left-hander to win three World Series games and the first pitcher since 1920 to win three games in a single World Series. His ERA for the series was a microscopic 0.45.

In 1948, Brecheen had the best year of his career. Early in the season, he threw 27 consecutive scoreless innings. By the time the season ended, he was 20-7 and led the National League in winning percentage, ERA, strike-outs and shut-outs.

The next year, he won 14 games. Over the next three seasons, he was a combined 23-20 and was waived by the Cardinals after the 1952 season. He spent a single season with the St. Louis Browns, pitching for former teammate Marty Marion, who was managing the Browns. But a 5-13 record at age 38 brought an end to his career. When the Browns relocated to Baltimore and became the Orioles, Brecheen spent the next 14 seasons with them as a coach.

Whitey Kurowski, Enos Slaughter, Marty Marion, Stan Musial
Sportsman's Park, 1946

Four triumphant Cardinals posed for photographers after their dramatic win in Game 7 of the World Series. That season, Slaughter and Musial returned from the service to jump-start the offense. Musial won his second batting title with a .365 average and Slaughter's 130 RBI were tops in the National League. In addition, the team's home attendance topped one million for the first time in franchise history. Cardinals fans had no way of knowing that this would be Musial's last World Series and that it would take 18 years for St. Louis to win another pennant.

Ted Wilks
Pitcher, 1944 - 1951

Ted Wilks was a starting pitcher who became a reliever after a tremendous rookie season.

Wilks got his shot at the majors because of the manpower shortage during the war. Rejected by the military because of a stomach ulcer, Wilks took his spot in the Cardinals' starting rotation after starting pitcher George Munger joined the service in the middle of 1944.

Wilks became an instant sensation. His 17-4 record marked the league's highest winning percentage and he threw more than 200 innings, including four shut-outs.

The next year, elbow problems limited Wilks to 16 starts and a 4-7 record. When the team's veteran pitchers returned from the war in 1946, Wilks was moved to the bullpen, where he thrived. Over the next three seasons, he went 18-6, all in relief. In 1949, he led the league in appearances and saves, while notching 10 victories. Arm problems cost him almost the entire 1950 season and early the next year, he was traded to the Pirates. There, he rebounded to again lead the National League in appearances and saves in 1951. He retired at age 37 following one final season with the Cleveland Indians.

Joe Garagiola
Catcher, 1946 - 1951

Joe Garagiola was the local boy who made good for the Cardinals. Yet despite a nine-year stint in the majors, he is best known for his career off the diamond.

Signed to a professional contract at age 16, Garagiola was called up at age 20 after returning from a two-year hitch with the Army in the Phillipines.

His first year, Garagiola saved his best effort for the postseason. In a two-game playoff against the Dodgers, his three hits and two RBI spurred a 4-2 Cardinals win in the first game. And when St. Louis advanced to the World Series against the Red Sox, Garagiola batted .316 with two doubles and four RBI.

Over the next three seasons, Garagiola shared catching duties with Del Rice. But in 1950, he separated his shoulder in a collision with Brooklyn Dodgers first baseman Jackie Robinson and missed more than half the season. The next spring, he was traded to the Pittsburgh Pirates, where he spent parts of three seasons. He later played with the Cubs and Giants before retiring after the 1954 season at age 28.

In 1955, Garagiola began a second career as a broadcaster. Putting his quick wit and playing experience to work, he returned to St. Louis to help broadcast Cardinals games. In 1961, he took over as the voice of NBC's *Game of the Week*, where he worked with Tony Kubek and Vin Scully for 28 years.

In 1969, Garagiola began a five-year run as host of *The Today Show*. He also authored several best-selling books on baseball and became a popular emcee on the banquet circuit for many years, entertaining listeners with humorous stories about life in the big leagues.

George "Red" Munger
Pitcher, 1943 - 1944; 1946 - 1952

Red Munger was a fire-balling right-hander and a consistent winner for the Cardinals, but his best season was interrupted by World War II.

In 1943, his first year with the Cardinals, Munger went 9-5. But the next year, he was headed for the record books in July, his record standing at 11-3 with an ERA of 1.34. And then the Army called.

Munger made it back for the end of the 1946 season and won Game 4 of the World Series before regaining his role in the St. Louis rotation in 1947. That season, his 16-5 record included 13 complete games and six shut-outs. Munger's last big season came in 1949 when he won 15 games. By 1950, arm problems began to lessen his effectiveness and he was traded to Pittsburgh during the 1952 season. Beginning in 1953, he pitched for the Hollywood Stars in the Pacific Coast League, where he won 23 games in 1955. He retired at age 38 following the 1957 season.

Del Rice
Catcher, 1945 - 1955; 1960

Del Rice spent 17 years as a catcher in the major leagues, but only four as an everyday player.

Rice grew up in the same Ohio neighborhood as Branch Rickey's brother Frank. Knowing all about him, Rickey signed the 18-year-old and sent him to the minors. Four years later, Rice joined the Cardinals as the team's back-up catcher. A gifted all-around athlete, he also played professional basketball for four years with the Rochester Royals of the National Basketball League.

Rice was never a great hitter, but his defensive skills and strong arm earned him a long career in the big leagues. In 1948, after being platooned for three seasons, Rice was given the starting job behind the plate. But his .197 batting average quickly cut his playing time in half.

Beginning in 1950, Rice became the Cardinals' regular catcher for four seasons. He never hit higher than .260 and his 11 home runs and 65 RBI in 1952 were career highs. In 1955, St. Louis traded Rice to the Milwaukee Braves, where he spent the next five years backing up Del Crandall. Rice later played for four different teams in his final two years in the majors, including a single game for the Cardinals in 1960. He retired after the 1961 season and spent six years as a coach in the American League before becoming a manager in the minor leagues. In 1972, Rice managed the California Angels for one season.

Howie Pollet
Pitcher, 1941 - 1943; 1946 - 1951

Howie Pollet was a two-time 20-game winner for the Cardinals.

Signed out of high school in New Orleans, Pollet first played for the Cardinals' minor-league team in Houston, where he twice won 20 games. Promoted to St. Louis in 1941, Pollet gradually moved into the Cardinals' starting rotation.

In 1943, Pollet was off to a great start with an 8-4 record and five shut-outs when he left to begin his military service. When he returned in 1946, he picked up where he left off. His 21-10 record and 2.10 ERA were tops in the National League. Chosen to start Game 1 of the 1946 World Series, Pollet threw 10 innings, but lost the game, 3-2, when he gave up a home run to Red Sox slugger Rudy York in the 10th inning.

Over the next two seasons, back and shoulder problems limited Pollet to a 22-19 record. Once healthy, Pollet again won 20 games in 1949. That season, his five shut-outs led the league.

Pollet was a finesse pitcher who relied on control to get batters out. Brooklyn Dodger Jackie Robinson called him "one of the toughest pitchers I ever faced." Pollet won 14 games in 1950 for St. Louis before he was traded to Pittsburgh early the next season. Though he would pitch in the majors for another six years, Pollet never won more than eight games in any single year. He retired after the 1956 season and entered the insurance business in Houston. In 1959, he returned to St. Louis as the Cardinals' pitching coach

Vernal "Nippy" Jones
First baseman, 1946 - 1951

Nippy Jones is best remembered for an incident that happened in his final at-bat in the major leagues.

In 1946, Jones joined the Cardinals' top farm team in Rochester after serving three years in the Marines. He batted .336 and finished second in the batting race to Montreal's Jackie Robinson who batted .337. Called up to St. Louis for the final month of the season, Jones went 4 for 12 before spending all but a month of the 1947 season back in the minors.

In 1948, Jones was installed as the Cardinals' first baseman so that Stan Musial could return to the outfield. Jones hit 10 home runs and his 81 RBI were third-highest on the team. In 1949, his final season as a regular, he batted .300. A back injury that year put Jones on the bench and kept him there for most of the rest of his career. In 1952, St. Louis traded him to the Phillies, but he spent the next four years in the minors. His final moment of glory came in the 1957 World Series while playing for the Milwaukee Braves.

In Game 4 against the Yankees, Jones was pinch hitting in the bottom of the 10th inning and Milwaukee was trailing, 5-4. When the pitcher's fourth pitch grazed Jones' shoe, he insisted that umpire Augie Donatelli check the ball. A black smudge of shoe polish convinced Donatelli that Jones had indeed been hit and he was awarded first base. The move kept the inning alive long enough for the Braves to tie the game and later, win it on a home run by Eddie Mathews. The victory evened the series and Milwaukee eventually defeated the Yankees in seven games. It was also the final game of Jones' career. He retired to Sacramento and later became a professional fishing guide.

Fred Saigh
Owner, 1947 - 1953

Following the Cardinals' second-place finish in 1947, team owner Sam Breadon decided to sell the franchise he had owned for nearly 30 years. Breadon was 71, in poor health and the value of the club appeared to be at an all-time high. With four National League pennants in six seasons, the team had drawn more than one million fans for the second consecutive year.

Fred Saigh (pronounced sigh) was a St. Louis attorney and businessman who owned a lot of downtown property. His partner in the purchase was former Postmaster General Robert Hannegan, a political friend of President Harry Truman. The duo paid Breadon a reported $4 million for the ball club and its 27 minor-league affiliates, borrowing heavily to finance the purchase. By 1949, Saigh bought out Hannegan's share for an additional $1 million.

The post-war economy of the United States was booming and fans were flocking to major-league ballparks in record numbers. And although the team never finished higher than second place during his reign, Saigh's Cardinals had four straight years where attendance surpassed one million. But huge debt payments meant revenues weren't reinvested in the ball club. In addition, the new Cardinals owner no longer had the luxury of Branch Rickey stockpiling talent in the minor leagues. As a result, the Cardinals floundered.

During his tenure, Saigh also made a conscious decision not to sign black ballplayers for St. Louis. Despite the arrival of Jackie Robinson in Brooklyn in 1947, and the obvious talents of Cleveland's Larry Doby and Boston's Sam Jethroe, no black player was signed by the Cardinals during Saigh's tenure as owner.

In the end, Saigh was convicted of income tax evasion in 1954 and sentenced to 15 months in prison. As a convicted felon, Saigh was summoned to New York by baseball Commissioner Happy Chandler and forced to sell the team.

Solly Hemus
Infielder, 1949 - 1956; 1959
Manager, 1959 - 1961

Solomon Hemus was a scrappy, hustling ballplayer whose uncanny ability to get on base endeared him to Cardinals fans everywhere.

Hemus had only an average arm and average speed, and at age 19, the Dodgers let him go because he showed so little promise. But after three years in the Navy, Hemus decided to give baseball another shot. Signed at a Cardinals try-out camp, he climbed the ranks on determination and will. His willingness to do whatever it took to win became his trademark. His teammates nicknamed him "Mighty Mouse."

Never a gifted hitter, Hemus took his job as the Cardinals' lead-off man seriously. He began crouching over the plate, daring pitchers to hit him. After all, his job was to get on base. During his four seasons as the Cardinals' regular shortstop, Hemus three times led the National League in being hit by a pitch. Brooklyn Dodger Pee Wee Reese noted that Hemus "crowds the plate until the pitcher doesn't have room to shed a tear."

Hemus' two best seasons came in 1952 and 1953, when he scored 105 and 110 runs respectively. In 1953, he also had 32 doubles, 11 triples and 14 home runs while batting .279. But the arrival of veteran shortstop Alvin Dark spelled the end for Hemus and he was traded to the Phillies early in 1956. In 1959, he was traded back to St. Louis and despite having never managed a single game, was named manager of the Cardinals. His best season was a third-place finish in 1960. But with the team in sixth place the next year, he was replaced by Johnny Keane. Hemus later served as a coach with the Mets and Indians.

Gerry Staley
Pitcher, 1947 - 1954

Sinkerball pitcher Gerry Staley was a consistent winner for the Cardinals during the early 1950s.

Staley joined the Cardinals after a three-year stint in the Army and some time in the minors perfecting his control. His first full year in St. Louis, he split time between the starting rotation and the bullpen. Over the next three seasons, he became the workhorse of the starting staff.

In 1951 and 1952, Staley was the only Cardinals pitcher to throw more than 200 innings. His 19 wins in 1951 were tops on the club. A two-time All-Star, Staley's best season came in 1953, when he went 18-9.

In 1954, Staley lost his effectiveness and won just seven games. He was traded to Cincinnati when the season ended. Staley spent the next two years with three different teams before landing with the Chicago White Sox in 1956. Used exclusively out of the bullpen, Staley became one of the most dependable relievers in the American League. It was a measure of his durability that Staley threw more than 100 innings of relief in three of his four full seasons in Chicago. In 1959, he led the league in appearances and in 1960, he won 13 games, all in relief. Staley retired after the 1961 season and coached for a single season with Portland in the Pacific Coast League.

Stan Musial and Warren Giles
Sportsman's Park, 1952

Midway through the 1952 season, Stan Musial was presented with a silver bat by National League President Warren Giles to commemorate his 1951 NL batting title. It was Musial's second consecutive batting crown and the fifth of his illustrious career. In addition, Musial was named Player of the Year by *The Sporting News*. His 205 hits in 1951 marked the fifth time he reached the coveted 200-hit plateau.

Musial would earn batting titles in 1952 and 1957, receiving seven by the time he ended his career.

Harvey Haddix
Pitcher, 1952 - 1956

Harvey Haddix is best remembered for throwing, and ultimately, losing the longest perfect game in major league history. But the greatest season of his long career was his first in St. Louis.

Though small in build, Haddix was a left-hander with a nasty curveball. His physical resemblance to former Cardinals pitcher Harry "the Cat" Brecheen earned him the nickname "Kitten." In 1953, his first full season with the Cardinals, Haddix won 20 games, threw a one-hitter and led the National League with six shut-outs. The next year, he notched 37 consecutive scoreless innings and 10 straight victories for a total of 18 wins.

Unfortunately, this was the high point of his career. Despite pitching 11 more years in the majors, Haddix never again won more than 13 games in a season. His 12-16 record with the Cardinals in 1955 got him traded to the Phillies the next year. After two mediocre years in Philadelphia and one in Cincinnati, Haddix was traded to the Pittsburgh Pirates for the 1959 season. There, he would enter the record books for a game he ended up losing.

On May 26, 1959, Haddix faced the Milwaukee Braves on the road. Squaring off with the Braves' Lew Burdette, Haddix retired 36 batters in a row. No pitcher in major-league history had ever thrown more than nine perfect innings and the longest hitless streak stood at 10 2/3 innings. Haddix eclipsed both. However, despite having 12 hits, the Pirates were held scoreless through 13 innings. When the first Braves batter reached base on a throwing error to begin the bottom of the 13th inning and Eddie Mathews was out sacrificing the runner to second, Haddix intentionally walked slugger Hank Aaron to set up a potential double play. But his bid for a no-hitter ended when the next batter, Joe Adcock, hit a home run over the centerfield wall to end the game with a Braves victory.

Haddix hung around for another six years with the Pirates and Orioles before retiring after the 1965 season. He later spent 13 years as a pitching coach in the majors with five different teams.

Albert "Red" Schoendienst
Second baseman, 1945 - 1956; 1961 - 1963

His five decades as a player, manager and coach with St. Louis allowed Red Schoendienst to spend more years in a Cardinals uniform than anyone else in team history.

Originally a shortstop in the minor leagues, the presence of veteran Marty Marion forced Schoendienst to spend his rookie season in the Cardinals' outfield. That season, his 28 stolen bases led the National League. Shifted to second base in 1946, Schoendienst's solid glove work anchored the right side of the Cardinals' infield for the next 10 seasons.

An eye injury as a teenager forced Schoendienst to become a switch-hitter while still in the minor leagues. As he developed at the plate, his power increased and in 1950, his 43 doubles led the league. In 1953, he batted .342 and hit a career-high 15 home runs. In 1954, he put together a 28-game hitting streak. But it was Schoendienst's defense that made him so valuable to St. Louis. His quickness and range made him a wiz at turning the double play.

But midway through the 1956 season, the 32-year-old Schoendienst was part of a nine-player trade with the New York Giants. A year later, he was traded again, this time to the Milwaukee Braves. There, Schoendienst helped the Braves to two World Series in 1957 and 1958. But a bout with tuberculosis cost Schoendienst nearly the entire 1959 season and effectively ended his career. Released by Milwaukee after the 1960 season, he returned for three seasons to St. Louis as a player-coach, where his 22 pinch hits in 1962 led the league. In 1965, Schoendienst embarked on a second career as manager of the Cardinals.

Eddie Stanky, Enos Slaughter, Gussie Busch, Red Schoendienst and Stan Musial
Spring Training, 1953

The income tax conviction of owner Fred Saigh forced the sale of the franchise early in 1953. Rumors that the Cardinals might leave St. Louis were published in the local press and the search for local buyers was on. Up stepped 54-year-old August "Gussie" Busch, Jr., the head of the Anheuser-Busch Brewing Company, the largest brewery in the United States. Busch convinced his board of directors to ratify the purchase of the Cardinals for $3.75 million dollars. His immense personal wealth and shrewd business sense convinced Busch that keeping the team in St. Louis was a matter of civic pride and a tremendous marketing opportunity.

Busch announced his purchase in February 1953 and headed to Florida to introduce himself to the team. In St. Louis, his first move was to renovate Sportsman's Park and rename it in his honor. By the 1960s, when the need for a new stadium was evident, Busch spearheaded the drive to build a multi-purpose stadium downtown. His ownership of the Cardinals franchise would stretch over four decades and eventually lead to five National League pennants and three World Series titles.

Harry Caray
Broadcaster, 1945 - 1969

For 25 years, Harry Caray was the voice of Cardinals baseball, but to get the job, he had to do some fast talking.

Caray came to St. Louis to host a late-night sports talk show. But when WTMV in East St. Louis posted an opening for a play-by-play man, Caray got an audience with the sponsor and pleaded to be put on the air. His enthusiasm and salesmanship landed him the job.

Like his rival Dizzy Dean, Caray was loud, opinionated and long on style and humor. For the next two years, Cardinals fans could listen to either of them. But in 1947, owner Sam Breadon made Caray and Street the exclusive radio announcers for Cardinals games. In 1953, Caray and the games moved to KMOX, where he was joined by Jack Buck the following year.

For the next 17 years, Caray's voice was heard in more than a dozen states over KMOX's booming signal, bringing legions of fans to the franchise and making Caray a household name.

In 1970, Caray left St. Louis and spent a single year in Oakland before migrating to Chicago, where he took over calling the White Sox games for the next 10 years. In 1981, he replaced Jack Brickhouse as the voice of the Cubs. Caray's trademark "Holy Cow!" and singing of "Take Me Out to the Ballgame" during the seventh-inning stretch became beloved traditions at Wrigley Field. Caray suffered a heart attack during spring training in 1999 and died at the age of 83.

Enos Slaughter
Sportsman's Park, 1954

Days before the season opener in 1954, 37-year-old Enos Slaughter was traded to the New York Yankees. Slaughter, who'd spent his entire 19-year career with the Cardinals, was reduced to tears by the news. He told assembled reporters, "This is the biggest shock of my life. I've given my life to this organization, and they let you go when they think you're getting old."

Slaughter spent six more seasons with New York and Kansas City before hanging it up after the 1959 season. He was elected to the Hall of Fame in 1985. In 1996, the Cardinals retired his uniform number 9.

Bill Virdon
Outfielder, 1955 - 1956

Bill Virdon was the National League's 1955 Rookie of the Year and gone from St. Louis a year later.

Virdon came to the Cardinals as part of the Enos Slaughter trade with New York. The Yankees had given up on the young outfielder because injuries and poor eyesight kept his batting average down. At the Cardinals' top minor-league club in Rochester, Virdon was persuaded to wear eyeglasses on the field and the impact was immediate. He won the International League batting title with a .333 average in 1954. The next spring, the Cardinals shifted Stan Musial back to first base to make room for Virdon in the outfield.

His rookie season, Virdon produced 17 home runs, 68 RBI and a .281 average. He put his high-school track-star skills to use patrolling centerfield at Sportsman's Park. But when he started off slowly the following April, he was traded to Pittsburgh for outfielder Bobby Del Greco and pitcher Dick Littlefield.

The trade was a disaster for the Cardinals. Del Greco was a weak-hitting outfielder who batted .215 in 102 games and was gone after one season. Littlefield was a journeyman left-hander who pitched three games before being traded a month later. With Pittsburgh, Virdon batted .334 his first season. Over the next nine years, he became a fixture in the Pirates outfield. In the 1960 World Series, his three doubles and five RBI helped fuel Pittsburgh's win over the Yankees. In 1962, he won a Gold Glove.

After retiring in 1968, Virdon began a long and distinguished career as a major-league manager and coach. He managed the Pirates to the 1972 NL pennant. His two years with the Yankees were followed by eight seasons as manager of the Houston Astros. Virdon spent two more years managing the Montreal Expos, before returning to Pittsburgh to coach for the Pirates.

Wally Moon
Outfielder, 1954 - 1958

The trade of Enos Slaughter just before opening day in 1954 left Cardinals fans outraged. But the arrival of 24-year-old rookie outfielder Wally Moon quickly eased their pain.

In his first major league at-bat, Moon hit a home run high over the right field wall at Sportsman's Park and onto Grand Avenue. By season's end, his .304 batting average and 193 hits earned him Rookie of the Year honors in the National League. Over the next three years, his average never dropped below .295 and in 1957, he hit 24 home runs and made the All-Star team.

The Cardinals tried moving Moon to first base his second season in St. Louis, but it was in right field that he made his reputation. His bushy eyebrows and matinee-idol looks made Moon a fan favorite. But injuries cost him nearly half the 1958 season and his batting average plummeted to .238. The Cardinals' front office panicked and sent Moon to the Los Angeles Dodgers for outfielder Gino Cimoli, who'd be gone a year later.

In Los Angeles, Moon took advantage of playing in the Los Angeles Coliseum, a converted football stadium more famous for hosting the Olympics. Despite the installation of a 42-foot-high screen in the stadium's left-field corner, the outfield wall remained only 250 feet away. Moon began hitting majestic home runs over the screen that fans began to call "Moon shots." In 1959, he hit 19 home runs and led the league with 11 triples. But after three seasons, the Dodgers moved to a new stadium and Moon's numbers fell dramatically. He spent another four years with the Dodgers, mostly as a reserve, before retiring after the 1965 season.

Moon returned home to Arkansas and briefly coached baseball at a nearby college. In 1976, he sold his home and put up his life savings to buy the Dodgers' minor-league team in San Antonio. But minor-league franchises were a money-losing proposition in the 1970s. Attendance was meager, the games weren't on local radio and Moon lost his shirt.

Tom Alston
First baseman, 1954 - 1957

In 1954, Tom Alston became the first African-American to play for the St. Louis Cardinals.

St. Louis purchased his contract for $100,000 from San Diego, where he'd just hit .297 with 23 home runs and 101 RBI. It was considered an enormous price in those days. But in an effort to boost his value, Alston and the Padres concealed his true age from St. Louis, claiming he was 23 instead of 28.

At six-foot-five, Alston cut an imposing figure and his defensive skills convinced the St. Louis front office that he would be a star. The Cardinals trumpeted his signing with a huge press conference presided over by team owner Gussie Busch. It had been seven years since Jackie Robinson broke baseball's color barrier and during that span, nine other clubs had signed a black player. Alston was greeted quietly by his new teammates.

In the third game of the 1954 season, Alston hit a home run. The next day, he came off the bench to hit another. He had no way of knowing that he would hit only two more home runs in the majors. By June, he was batting .244 and was sent to Rochester to regain his stroke. Over the next three seasons, he was shuttled back and forth between St. Louis and the minors. With Stan Musial stationed at first base in 1955, there really was no place for Alston and so he saw only 27 more at-bats for the Cardinals.

His on-field struggles soon became overshadowed by his off-field problems. In the minors, Alston began hearing voices. Back home in North Carolina, he attempted suicide after the 1957 season. The Cardinals sent Alston to a psychiatrist who diagnosed him with a nervous disorder and treated him with electro-shock therapy. The team urged him to enter a mental hospital, but he refused. Released by the Cardinals in 1959, Alston returned home, broke and alone. Two days later, he burned down a neighborhood church and was arrested. For the next 10 years, he was confined to a mental institution. When he was released in 1969, he lived with his sister in Greensboro for 18 years and scraped by on disability payments. For the next five years, Alston lived by himself in a tiny apartment before dying of prostate cancer in 1993.

Don Blasingame
Second baseman, 1955 - 1959

Speedy Don Blasingame was considered such a sure thing that the Cardinals traded veteran Red Schoendienst to the Giants to make room at second base for the 24-year-old rookie. In fact, Blasingame had been the American Association's Rookie of the Year in 1955 when he batted .302 for Omaha.

Blasingame's skill as a bunter and speed on the bases quickly earned him the lead-off position in the Cardinals' batting order and the nickname "the Blazer." He twice stole more than 20 bases in a single season for St. Louis. Yet his greatest strength was his ability to cover a lot of ground on defense. Blasingame's glove routinely robbed batters of sure hits. His skill at the plate was equally valuable. He proved especially adept at spoiling opposing pitchers' no-hit bids, breaking up four in late innings.

It was the impending arrival of rookie Julian Javier that got Blasingame traded to San Francisco after the 1959 season. After that, Blasingame became a nomad, playing for four different teams in the next seven seasons. In 1966, at age 34, his career in the majors was over. Blasingame spent the next 16 years playing and managing in Japan. In 1983, he returned to the Cardinals as a roving minor-league instructor.

Alex Grammas
Infielder, 1954 - 1956; 1959 - 1962

Alex Grammas' glove got him to the majors, but his weak bat kept him from becoming an everyday player for much of his career.

In 1953, Grammas batted .304 for Kansas City and led the American Association in put-outs and assists. The Cardinals were so impressed that they spent $100,000 to buy his contract. But Grammas batted a disappointing .252 his first two seasons in St. Louis and was promptly traded to Cincinnati. In 1959, he returned to the Cardinals as the team's regular shortstop, hitting .269 with a career-high 30 RBI. But a declining batting average cut his playing time and by 1961, he was a reserve. Traded the next season, Grammas spent one year with the Cubs before retiring.

In 1965, Grammas began a second career as a major-league coach with the Pirates. After five years in Pittsburgh, he spent six years in Cincinnati under Manager Sparky Anderson. In 1976, he managed the Milwaukee Brewers for two losing seasons before re-joining Anderson in Detroit for another 11 years.

Wilmer "Vinegar Bend" Mizell
Pitcher, 1952 - 1953; 1956 - 1960

Vinegar Bend Mizell was a big old country boy from the rural South who struggled to control his blazing fastball.

Mizell was nicknamed after the tiny Alabama town, population 37, where he first threw a baseball. Signed by a Cardinals scout at age 18, he blazed his way through the minor leagues. In 1950, he struck out 227 batters in 207 innings for Winston-Salem and in 1951, he led the Texas league with 257 strike-outs, including a record 18 in one game. That same season, in a promotional gimmick arranged by the Houston ball club, the entire population of Vinegar Bend boarded a bus and traveled to Houston to watch Mizell pitch.

When he arrived in St. Louis in 1952, the team's front office was bragging that Mizell was a faster, left-handed version of the great Dizzy Dean. But Mizell soon discovered that speed wasn't enough to win in the big leagues. He went 10-8 his rookie season, but also led the National League in walks. He simply couldn't harness his control long enough to justify the hype. Following a 13-11 record in 1953, Mizell spent the next two years in the military. Upon his return in 1956, he won a career high 14 games, including three shut-outs. But in July 1957, he injured his arm in Milwaukee when he slipped on the mound after a long rain delay. Arm and shoulder problems continued to plague him and finally, in 1960, the Cardinals traded him to Pittsburgh for two minor-leaguers.

With the Pirates, Mizell went 13-5 over the remainder of the season and helped pitch Pittsburgh to their first World Series in more than 30 years. It was also his last winning season in the majors. He retired after the 1962 season. In 1968, Mizell was elected to Congress, where he served three terms as a Republican from Mississippi.

Ken Boyer
Polo Grounds, 1955

Ken Boyer was the greatest third baseman in the history of the St. Louis Cardinals. His outstanding defense and consistent run production were the trademark of his 11 seasons in St. Louis.

Raised in a family that produced three major leaguers, Boyer signed with the Cardinals out of high school for $6,000. After three years in the minors and two in the military, Boyer had a break-out year for Houston in 1954. He batted .318, notched 202 hits and produced 21 home runs and 116 RBI. The Cardinals' front office, tired of the constant turnover at third base, gave Boyer the job the next spring.

Deceptively quick, Boyer stole 22 bases his rookie year and played flawless defense. In 1956, he batted .306 and his 26 home runs and 98 RBI were second best on the team behind Stan Musial. At the plate, Boyer was amazingly consistent. Starting in 1958, he had seven straight years with at least 20 home runs and 90 RBI. He batted over .300 five times. In 1959, he put together a 29-game hitting streak, the longest run in the majors in nine years.

However, Boyer's quiet personality caused him problems. He played hurt and he played hard, but frequently, he was booed by fans who expected him to be a more vocal leader. Early in his career, Boyer feuded with general manager Frank Lane and in 1957, he was moved to centerfield for a single season. When he hit just .265 that year, Boyer was the subject of frequent trade rumors. Lane's departure to Cleveland kept Boyer in St. Louis where he soon helped lead the Cardinals back to the World Series.

On the field, Boyer became recognized as the finest defensive third baseman in the National League. He was a five-time Gold Glove winner and led NL third basemen in double-plays five times. His quick reflexes and ability to make spectacular plays look routine made him a seven-time All-Star. In 1963, he hit 24 home runs and knocked in a team-high 111 runs. But the best was yet to come.

Larry Jackson
Pitcher, 1955 - 1962

Larry Jackson was the workhorse of the Cardinals pitching staff for six seasons, but he had his best years before and after his tenure in St. Louis.

Jackson's second year in the minor leagues was one for the record books. Pitching for Fresno in 1952, he went 28-4, threw 30 complete games and struck out 351 batters in 300 innings.

In 1955, Jackson was promoted to the majors as part of the Cardinals' youth movement. He joined fellow rookies Ken Boyer and Bill Virdon, who were brought onboard to improve the club's sixth-place finish the previous year.

Used primarily in relief his first two years, Jackson went 15-9 as a starter in 1957. Over the next five seasons, he went 75-61 for a team that finished higher than fourth only once. Jackson's greatest talent was his ability to eat up a lot of innings. Four times he led the Cardinals pitching staff in innings pitched. In 1960, he won 18 games and led the National League in starts. But following a 16-win season in 1962, Jackson was traded to the lowly Chicago Cubs.

In Chicago, Jackson joined a team that had produced 11 straight losing seasons and not surprisingly, he suffered from poor run support. In 1963, he went 14-18 for the Cubs, despite having the sixth-lowest ERA in the National League. In his 18 losses, the Cubs scored a total of 29 runs and Jackson lost three games by a score of 1-0. In 1964, Jackson finally put together his greatest season. He led the league with 24 wins, including a one-hitter against the Reds. Only a single by Pete Rose kept Jackson from throwing a perfect game.

Traded to the Phillies in 1966 for Ferguson Jenkins, Jackson retired after the 1968 season. He returned to Idaho and served four terms in the state legislature. Jackson died of cancer in 1990 at age 59.

Lindy McDaniel
Pitcher, 1955 - 1962

Lindy McDaniel spent more than 20 years pitching in the major leagues, but only two seasons as a starter.

The Cardinals signed McDaniel for $50,000 in 1955 and rushed the 19-year-old to the majors. He joined St. Louis without spending a day in the minor leagues.

McDaniel spent most of his first two seasons in the bullpen, but became a starter in 1957. He responded with a 15-9 record as the surprising Cardinals finished in second place. But both McDaniel and the Cardinals slumped badly the next year and the young right-hander found himself shipped to the minor leagues.

There, McDaniel changed his delivery and again began pitching out of the bullpen. When he returned to St. Louis in 1959, he quickly became one of the best relievers in the league. In 1960, he was chosen Fireman of the Year by *The Sporting News*. He led the National League in saves for two straight years. But in 1961, his ERA suddenly doubled and he lost his effectiveness. After the 1962 season, the Cardinals traded him to the Cubs.

The move proved premature as McDaniel rebounded to again lead the league in saves. Over the next 12 seasons, he pitched for three different teams, all in relief. In 1968, with the New York Yankees, he retired 32 consecutive batters. In 1970, he earned a career-high 29 saves. When he retired after the 1975 season, his 987 career appearances as a pitcher ranked him number two on baseball's all-time list.

Ernie Broglio
Pitcher, 1959 - 1964

Pitcher Ernie Broglio was a 20-game winner with St. Louis whose value was measured in an historic trade.

Broglio was in the minor leagues when San Francisco traded him to the Cardinals after the 1958 season. His rookie year in St. Louis, he struggled to a 7-12 record, but manager Solly Hemus was patient with the young right-hander and was rewarded with a 21-win season in 1960.

Broglio began that season in the bullpen, but the Cardinals were desperate for starters and called on his resilient right arm to start and relieve. Despite only five wins by late June, Broglio became almost unstoppable during the second half of the season. On July 15, he threw a one-hitter against the Cubs while striking out 14. He went 16-5 the rest of the way and was at his best against the National League's strongest teams, defeating the pennant-winning Pirates all

four times he faced them and beating the Braves five times in seven tries.

But shoulder problems limited Broglio to nine victories in 1961. His 1962 season included four shut-outs and back-to-back two-hitters. Finally healthy in 1963, his 18-8 record was tops on the staff. However, early in the 1964 season, the Cardinals traded Broglio to the Cubs in a multi-player deal that brought 24-year-old Lou Brock to St. Louis. The deal proved the defining moment in both players' careers.

In Chicago, Broglio's arm problems returned and he won just seven games in three years. He was forced to retire after the 1966 season. Brock, who'd struggled at the plate during his two seasons in Chicago, caught fire and batted .348 for the rest of the year. His blinding speed and keen batting eye would carry him to a Hall of Fame career in 15 seasons for the Cardinals.

Curt Flood
Outfielder, 1958 - 1969

Curt Flood played ball for the same high school in Oakland, California, that produced Frank Robinson and Vada Pinson. All three were signed by the Cincinnati Reds and each would go on to star in the National League. But the Reds later traded Flood to the Cardinals for three mediocre pitchers, making one of the worst trades in their history.

Only 20, Flood eventually became one of the game's finest defensive outfielders. His acrobatic catches earned him seven consecutive Gold Glove awards. At the plate, he slowly learned to cut down his swing and drive the ball to all fields. In 1961, he batted .322. But his career really took off when he began batting lead-off for St. Louis. In 1964, his 211 hits led the league and he collected eight straight hits in a double-header against the Dodgers.

Unfortunately, it was a fielding blunder in the 1968 World Series that most Cardinals fans choose to remember about Flood. In Game 7 against the Tigers, with the teams knotted in a scoreless tie after six innings, he misjudged a fly ball that sailed over his head for a triple, scoring two runs. Detroit eventually won the game 4-1 and Flood was the goat. He played another season for St. Louis before the Cardinals traded him to the Phillies after the 1969 season. Flood's response to the trade would shock baseball to its foundations and fundamentally change the game forever.

Bill White
First baseman, 1959 - 1965; 1969

Bill White was a smooth-fielding first baseman whose booming bat helped power the Cardinals' offense in the early 1960s.

His career ended in baseball's front office, but began as a rookie sensation with the New York Giants. During his first trip to the plate, he hit a home run. By the time the season ended, he had hit 22. But the military interrupted his career and in 1959, the Giants traded him to the Cardinals.

His first year in St. Louis, playing left field, White made the All-Star team. Moved to first base the next season, his defensive skills shined through. His quick hands and agile feet earned him seven consecutive Gold Glove awards.

At the plate, White abandoned his uppercut swing and began hitting line drives to all fields. For six straight seasons, he hit at least 20 home runs. Unlike most sluggers, he also could hit for average. In 1961, he put together 14 consecutive hits in back-to-back double-headers against the Cubs, tying the major-league record set by Ty Cobb. The humble White downplayed his accomplishment, telling reporters, "The best thing is that we won four games in two days."

In 1962, White batted .324 and drove in 102 runs. It would be the first of three consecutive years with more than 100 RBI. When St. Louis won the NL pennant in 1964, White contributed 21 home runs, 102 RBI and a .303 average.

In 1965, the Cardinals' poor showing led to wholesale roster changes and White was traded to the Phillies. He had one last great season in 1966 before his batting average and power numbers fell dramatically. In 1969, he returned to the Cardinals as a pinch-hitter before retiring at season's end. In 1971, White joined Phil Rizzuto in the Yankees' broadcast booth for 18 years before being named president of the National League in 1989, a position he held for five years.

Ray Sadecki
Pitcher, 1960 - 1966; 1975

Ray Sadecki's best season helped propel the Cardinals to their first National League title in 18 years.

As a youngster, Sadecki showed so much promise that the Cardinals offered him a $50,000 signing bonus. But from the start, he had trouble controlling his fastball. He led the American Association in walks his second year in the minors, despite being second in strike-outs.

Eager for a return on their investment, the Cardinals rushed Sadecki to the majors at age 19. The next year, he won 14 games and led the fifth-place team in innings pitched, but struggled to keep the ball in the park. In 1963, he led the pitching staff in home runs allowed and struggled to a 10-10 record.

In 1964, at age 24, Sadecki finally fulfilled expectations and put together the best year of his career. Although he didn't win his first game until May 11, he grew strong down the stretch, throwing back-to-back shut-outs in September and defeating the Cardinals' two main rivals, the Reds and Phillies. He became only the franchise's fourth left-hander to win 20 games and the first since 1949. He benefited from the Cardinals' suddenly potent offense. The team's .272 batting average led the league and the Cardinals placed second in runs scored. In the World Series against the Yankees, Sadecki won Game 1, but failed to complete the first inning of Game 4, giving New York three runs before being pulled from a game the Cardinals rallied to win, 4-3.

The next year, the Cardinals' offense went sour and so did Sadecki. His ERA ballooned to 5.21. He again led the staff in giving up the long ball and he finished a dismal 6-15. Early the next season, the Cardinals traded him to the Giants for slugger Orlando Cepeda. Despite pitching for another 11 years in the majors, Sadecki never won more than 12 games a year. In 1968, his 18 losses led the league and eventually he was moved to the bullpen. Sadecki pitched in eight games for the 1975 Cardinals, then played for four other teams before retiring in 1977.

Bob Gibson
Spring Training, 1960

With all the accolades bestowed upon Bob Gibson, it is difficult for Cardinals fans to remember that the franchise's greatest pitcher wasn't an immediate success.

Gibson overcame a sickly childhood and poverty to become one of the game's most dominating pitchers. His father died before he was born and while growing up in Omaha, Gibson suffered from asthma and rickets. Standing less than five feet tall as a freshman at Omaha's Tech High, he developed into a two-sport star. However, his dream of playing hoops for Indiana University ended when he received a letter that read, "Your request for an athletic scholarship has been denied because we have already filled our quota of Negroes." Instead, he attended nearby Creighton University, where he was the basketball team's only black player and also pitched for the baseball team.

When he graduated in 1957, Gibson signed professional contracts with the St. Louis Cardinals and the Harlem Globetrotters. Married at 21, he wanted to supplement his $4,000 signing bonus from the Cardinals with some off-season basketball paychecks. But after one year of playing both sports, Gibson was persuaded to concentrate strictly on baseball.

His first two years in the minors, Gibson went a mediocre 14-13 and walked nearly as many batters as he struck out. In 1959, he began shuttling back and forth between the minors and the majors. In his first starting assignment in St. Louis, Gibson shut out the Reds, 1-0, but he pitched infrequently and recorded only a 6-11 record over two seasons.

Gibson's fortunes improved when Johnny Keane replaced Solly Hemus as Cardinals manager midway through the 1961 season. Keane had been Gibson's manager during his two seasons in the minors and believed in the skinny right-hander's talent. Keane assured Gibson of a spot in the starting rotation.

Early on, Gibson couldn't seem to avoid giving up runs at the start of a game. During one stretch in 1961, he allowed first-inning runs in eight of nine starts. That same season, at age 25, he led the National League in walks, but managed to win 13 games, throw 10 complete games and two shut-outs. When Gibson notched 208 strike-outs and five shut-outs in 1962, he was finally on his way.

Tim McCarver
Catcher, 1959 - 1961; 1963 - 1969; 1973 - 1974

Tim McCarver spent 21 years behind the plate — strong on defense, steady with the bat and a skilled partner for some of the league's best pitchers.

McCarver made his debut at age 17 after the Cardinals gave him a $75,000 signing bonus to win a bidding war. The Memphis high school star ripped up the Midwest League with a .360 average and was rushed to the majors for a late-season look in 1959. Three brief trials in St. Louis proved McCarver was overmatched at the plate, so he spent the 1962 season in Atlanta perfecting his game. The next year, he came back to St. Louis as the Cardinals' starting catcher.

Although a career .271 hitter, McCarver never produced gaudy power stats. His highest value was his confidence in handling a pitching staff and his excellent defensive skills. He was an aggressive leader on the field and an outgoing personality in the clubhouse. He wasn't afraid to challenge veteran pitchers Bob Gibson and Steve Carlton, while delighting teammates with practical jokes and impersonations. A career highlight came in the 1964 World Series against the Yankees, when he batted .478 and his three-run homer in the 10th inning won Game 5 for St. Louis.

In 1970, McCarver was traded to the Phillies, where he spent parts of three seasons before briefly rejoining St. Louis in 1973. In 1975, he was reunited with former battery mate Steve Carlton in Philadelphia. The duo became inseparable on the field as McCarver became Carlton's personal catcher. Over the next five years, he helped Carlton win 20 games three times.

When McCarver retired in 1980, he began a distinguished second career as a television sports broadcaster.

Vaughn "Bing" Devine
General Manager, 1958 - 1964; 1968 - 1978

Bing Devine made some of the most significant trades in Cardinals history.

Devine became a master of the deal after succeeding Frank Lane as general manager and inheriting a team whose farm system had fallen into disarray. His first trade secured the unproven Curt Flood from Cincinnati. And in 1964, he stole a young Lou Brock from the Cubs as the Cardinals won their first title in 18 years.

The next year, Devine left to run the New York Mets, but returned in 1968 and began overhauling the roster. His trade of Orlando Cepeda to Atlanta for Joe Torre in 1969 was well-timed.

However, not all of his deals turned out well. His decision to trade a disgruntled Steve Carlton to the Phillies ranks as probably the worst deal in team history. But it was his failure to win a division title over the next 10 years that ultimately cost Devine his job in 1978.

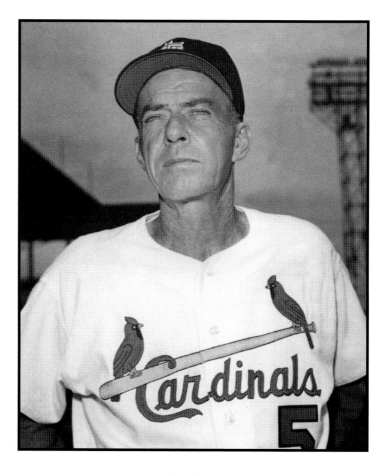

Johnny Keane
Manager, 1961 - 1964

Johnny Keane spent 31 years as a player, coach and manager in the Cardinals' minor-league system before succeeding Solly Hemus as manager midway through the 1961 season.

Keane took over a sixth-place team and gradually led St. Louis to a second-place finish in 1963. But the firing of Bing Devine in 1964 rubbed Keane wrong. That season, when the Cardinals started slowly, rumors began circulating that owner Gussie Busch was looking for a new manager. Keane kept quiet and bided his time. When the team caught fire and raced to a title during the final two months of the season, Busch offered Keane a new contract. Keane put him off, preferring to concentrate on the upcoming World Series against the New York Yankees, which the Cardinals won in seven games. At a press conference the next day, Keane surprised everyone by resigning. He was immediately hired as the new manager of the Yankees, replacing the recently ousted Yogi Berra. Keane lasted only 20 games into the 1966 season as the Yankees suffered their worst two seasons in four decades.

Bob Gibson
Pitcher, 1959 - 1975

Not even a broken leg could stop Bob Gibson from becoming the Cardinals' ace.

Late in 1962, Gibson's spikes caught in the ground during batting practice and he broke his fibula. The injury ended his season with 15 wins. The next year, he came back strong, going 18-9. And over the next three years, his victories steadily increased — from 19 in 1964, to 20 in 1965, to 21 in 1966. His consecutive 20-win seasons were the first by a Cardinals pitcher in 21 years.

As Gibson matured, he became more of a pitcher and less of a thrower. Although his stock in trade was a blinding fastball, he began to effectively mix in a slider and a curveball. He gradually was able to reduce the number of pitches he threw, which allowed him to finish more games. Gibson had 20 complete games in 1965 and 1966. Yet as he reduced his number of walks, he remained among the league's leaders in strike-outs.

Gibson's no-nonsense approach and his inside pitches got him labeled a "headhunter." He was unapologetic, stating, "If you're going to worry about hitting a guy, then you're not supposed to be out on the mound. I made my living pitching inside so I could pitch away when I wanted to." When batters crowded the plate, he would quickly re-establish his claim to both sides of the dish. Even friends weren't immune. When former roommate Bill White returned to St. Louis with the Phillies the next season, Gibson recalled, "I told him if either of us ever got traded, and he hit my pitch out there, I'd hit him on the arm. He fouled off an outside pitch, and I hit him on the elbow with the next one. He and I were close, but when he was on the other club, I had to win."

The result was a public persona that many thought cold and aloof. Gibson reminded reporters, "I don't care if people like me. I want people to respect me. I want them to know me as a competitor, to know that I gave 100 percent every time."

Gibson suffered a second broken leg in 1967 when he was struck by a ball off the bat of Pirates great Roberto Clemente. He missed six weeks and had to settle for a 13-7 record. But he recovered in time to shut down the Boston Red Sox in three World Series starts. He struck out 26 batters in 27 innings and allowed only 14 hits. He had an ERA of 1.00 as St. Louis won its second championship in four years. Remarkably, Gibson's 1968 season would be even better.

Mike Shannon
Outfielder, Third baseman; 1962 - 1970

Medical problems cut short Mike Shannon's major league career, but his eight seasons with the Cardinals were highlighted by great moments in the postseason.

Shannon was a gifted all-around athlete who gave up a football scholarship at the University of Missouri to concentrate on baseball. The switch meant five long years in the minor leagues before he was given a brief trial in St. Louis in 1962. His strong arm and hustling style got him into the everyday lineup by the middle of the 1964 season. And when the Cardinals rallied to win 35 of their final 50 games and capture the National League pennant, it was Shannon's bat that led the way. His clutch hitting and 43 RBI in the final two months of the season made the difference. In Game 1 of the World Series against the Yankees, Shannon's two-run home run tied the game, which St. Louis eventually won, 9-5.

Shannon became the Cardinals' everyday right fielder in 1965 and hit a career-high 16 home runs the next season. In 1967, he was asked to move to third base to make room for newly acquired outfielder Roger Maris. Shannon's natural talent served him well as he learned a new position at the major league level. In the 1967 World Series, he hit another two-run homer to give St. Louis a 5-2 win in Game 3. In 1968, his career-high 79 RBI helped the Cardinals reach their second straight World Series. But his homer in Game 7 was the Cardinals' only run as the Detroit Tigers took the series.

During spring training in 1970, Shannon was diagnosed with a severe kidney disorder. He played in only 52 games before doctors told him he was through. In 1972, Shannon joined veteran Jack Buck in the Cardinals' broadcast booth at KMOX. Over the next 30 years, Shannon's off-beat comments became legendary as the duo entertained Cardinals fans throughout the Midwest.

Julian Javier
Second baseman, 1960 - 1971

Julian Javier's speed and snaring glove made him a fixture in the Cardinals' infield for more than a decade.

One of the game's first Dominican players, the Cardinals acquired Javier from Pittsburgh in return for veteran pitcher Vinegar Bend Mizell. Javier brought tremendous range and an ability to turn the difficult double play. Although he never became a big run producer, his lifetime .257 average and speed on the base paths ignited the Cardinals' offense. His job was to get on base in front of the sluggers. In 1962, his third season in the majors, he scored 97 runs and stole 26 bases. After missing half of the 1965 season to injuries, he hit .281 and belted a career-high 14 home runs in 1967.

But Javier's lasting value to St. Louis was in the field. Over 11 full seasons, he solidified a position that had seen steady turnover since the departure of Red Schoendienst in 1956. Javier excelled at making the tough play. He routinely corralled short pop flies and went deep behind second base to begin double plays.

In 1966, another Latin ballplayer, Orlando Cepeda, arrived and helped the reserved Javier on and off the field. As his English improved, Javier became more outgoing and Cepeda worked with him on his hitting. In the 1967 World Series, Javier batted .360 with three doubles and a home run in Game 7. But injuries slowed Javier and in 1971, St. Louis traded him to the Reds for pitcher Tony Cloninger. Javier retired the next year at age 36.

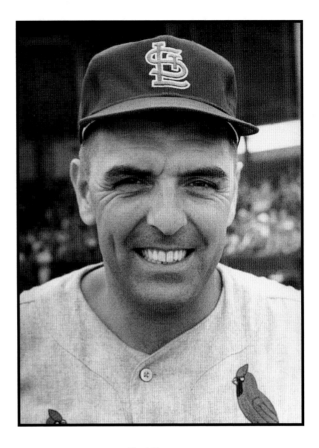

Curt Simmons
Pitcher, 1960 - 1966

Lefty Curt Simmons found new life and a second career in St. Louis after the Phillies released him in 1960.

Simmons had been a consistent winner during 12 seasons in Philadelphia. In 1950, his 17-8 record helped pace the Phillies to their first National League pennant in 35 years. But arm problems in 1958 slowed his legendary fastball and he ended the year at 7-14. When he threw only 10 innings the next season, it appeared his career was over at age 30. But St. Louis was desperate for pitching help and willing to take a chance on a sore-armed veteran who hadn't won a game in almost two years.

With the Cardinals, Simmons overhauled his delivery, began relying on off-speed pitches and started winning games. In his first two-plus years in St. Louis, he went 26-24. But in 1963, he won 15 games and threw six shut-outs.

In 1964, Simmons went 18-9 and won six straight down the stretch to help the Cardinals overtake his old team. In fact, against the Phillies, Simmons was 16-2 while with the Cardinals. But 1964 was his last good year. After he went 9-15 in 1966, the Cardinals traded him to the Cubs the next year. He retired after the 1967 season and began running a golf course in the Philadelphia area.

Dick Groat
Shortstop, 1963 - 1965

Veteran Dick Groat's strong bat and experience helped lead the Cardinals to the 1964 National League pennant.

Groat came from Pittsburgh, where in 1960, he won a batting title and was named the league's Most Valuable Player. His first season in St. Louis, he batted .319, amassed 201 hits and led the league with 43 doubles.

More importantly, he teamed with Julian Javier to give the Cardinals their most athletic double-play tandem in two decades. Groat's knowledge of opposing hitters helped him position the St. Louis infielders for better defense. In 1964, the entire Cardinals' infield was selected to the All-Star team.

Groat was a leader in the clubhouse and played in 161 of the team's 162 games in 1964. But following a sub-par year in 1965, he was traded to the Phillies during a team housecleaning. He spent one full season in Philadelphia before finishing with the Giants in 1967.

Stan Musial
Sportsman's Park, September 29, 1963

By 1963, Stan Musial was 42 and no longer playing every day. It had been six years since his last great season, when he drove in more than 100 runs and hit .351 to win his seventh batting title. Age and injuries were taking their toll. Rumors of his retirement dogged Musial as early as 1959, when his batting average slumped to .255 and he was benched for the last six weeks of the season. But his status as the team's icon and an annual salary of $100,000 kept him going. He rallied in 1962 for one last time, batting .330 and knocking in 82 runs, his best in five years. But early in August 1963, Musial held a press conference to announce he would retire at the end of the season.

Musial played his last game on September 29, 1963, at home against the Cincinnati Reds. At a pre-game ceremony at home plate, Musial was surrounded by family, teammates and Commissioner Ford Frick, who spoke for all baseball fans, noting, "Here stands baseball's perfect warrior. Here stands baseball's perfect knight." Musial's number six was retired by team owner Gussie Busch who said, "No one could do justice to it." Musial took a convertible ride around the ballpark and then took his place on the field.

A single in the fourth inning and another in the sixth marked the final hits of his illustrious career. To the thunderous roar of the crowd, he was taken out of the game for a pinch runner. In the clubhouse, reporters and photographers crowded around his locker. Musial slowly removed his uniform for the last time and told the assembled group, "You know that's the way I came in. Two base hits. And that's the way I leave."

Musial's career statistics rank among the greatest in the game. His 3,630 hits are fourth on baseball's all-time list and the most ever by a Cardinal. His 6,134 total bases are second only to Hank Aaron. He is the all-time team leader in almost every offensive category, including walks, doubles, triples, home runs, RBI and runs scored. He played in 3,026 games for St. Louis, a mark that will never be equaled.

Stan Musial was elected to the Hall of Fame in 1969.

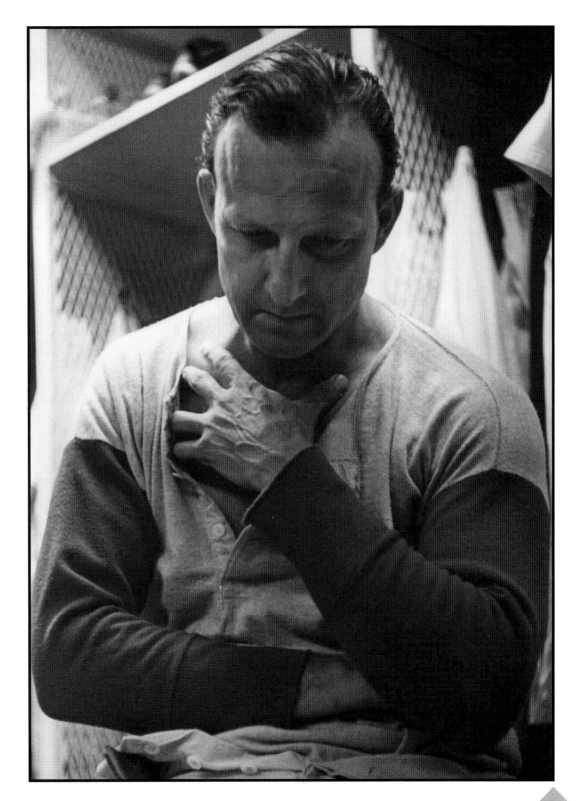

Dal Maxvill
Shortstop, 1962 - 1972
Executive, 1985 - 1994

Dal Maxvill's defensive skills kept him in the majors for parts of 14 seasons, but his weakness at the plate was legendary.

Signed by the Cardinals out of college for $1,000, Maxvill spent three years in the minors, where his glove got him noticed. By 1962, he was in the majors as a back-up infielder, but he was shipped back to the minors for most of the 1964 season because he couldn't produce at the plate. However, a late-season injury to Julian Javier brought him back for the stretch run. Maxvill played second base in all seven games of the World Series, batted .200 and played solid defense.

When veteran shortstop Dick Groat was traded to the Phillies after the 1965 season, a regular spot opened up for Maxvill. Still, he continued to struggle at the plate. In 1967, he batted .227 and his meager 41 RBI were a career-high. But in the field, he came to be recognized as one of the league's premier shortstops. In 1968, he earned a Gold Glove award. Yet in the World Series against the Tigers, Maxvill set a record for futility by going 0 for 22 at the plate. The next year, he became the answer to a trivia question when, during a game in Montreal, he hit the first regular-season home run ever produced outside the United States.

In 1970, his problems at the plate intensified. His 80 hits and 89 total bases set a record as fewest in a season by someone who played in at least 150 games. Late in 1972, the Cardinals traded Maxvill to the Oakland A's, where he spent parts of three seasons before retiring in 1975 with a career .217 average. He spent the next seven seasons as a coach with four different major league teams.

In 1985, Maxvill became the surprise pick as the Cardinals' new general manager. He began overseeing the team assembled by manager Whitey Herzog, who received most of the credit for the two National League pennants in 1985 and 1987. The death of team owner Gussie Busch in 1989 ended the team's free-spending ways and Herzog's departure in 1990 left Maxvill alone at the helm. Maxvill brought in Joe Torre as manager and although the Cardinals posted winning records in each of the next three seasons, the lack of a pennant frustrated fans. Late in the 1994 season, during the baseball strike, Maxvill was fired.

Bobby Shantz, Curt Flood, Bill White and Ken Boyer
Sportsman's Park, 1964

Throughout the 1960s, the Cardinals were known for their terrific defense. Each of the four players above, shown receiving their 1963 Gold Glove awards before a May home game, were multiple winners. Pitcher Bobby Shantz, who spent just two-plus seasons with the Cardinals, won the award twice. Outfielder Curt Flood won seven straight Gold Gloves starting in 1963. First baseman Bill White won the award six years straight starting in 1960. And third baseman Ken Boyer was a five-time winner. Combined with pitcher Bob Gibson's five trophies, Cardinals players were awarded 24 Gold Gloves during the decade.

Lou Brock
Outfielder, 1964 - 1979

The trade that brought Lou Brock to St. Louis midway through 1964 marked the turning point in the Cardinals' championship season.

The Chicago Cubs had had lofty expectations for Brock. During his one season in the minors, he produced huge numbers and was named the Northern League's Player of the Year. In the majors, however, he was overmatched. His first two years in Chicago, Brock's talent was overshadowed by his weak bat and poor play in the outfield. During day games at windy Wrigley Field, he often misplayed routine fly balls or threw to the wrong base. By 1964, the Cubs' front office was losing faith in the speedy 24-year-old.

St. Louis had noticed Brock the previous July when he hit two home runs and a triple in a game against the Cardinals. Wanting to shake up a fourth-place team with a 28-30 record, management sent veteran pitcher Ernie Broglio to the Cubs for Brock, a trade that Cardinals fans met with skepticism. After all, Broglio had won 21 games in 1960 and 18 in 1963. It seemed a lopsided trade for an unproven outfielder. But the change in scenery jumpstarted Brock's career and the Cardinals' pennant hopes.

Cardinals manager Johnny Keane told Brock that he would play every day only if he began to steal bases. Brock, who thought of himself as a power hitter, initially objected. But Keane was adamant and Brock soon put his speed on display. Almost immediately, every facet of his game improved. Over the last four months of the season, Brock batted .348 and finished with 200 hits, 30 doubles, 14 home runs and 43 stolen bases. He proved a catalyst as the team went 65-39 the rest of the season and won their first National League pennant in 18 years. In the World Series against the Yankees, Brock hit .300 with a home run and 5 RBI. For Cardinals fans, the best part was that Brock was just getting started.

Ken Boyer
Third baseman, 1955 - 1965

In 1964, veteran Ken Boyer had the best offensive year of his career. He hit a team-high 24 home runs and a league-leading 119 RBI. He whacked 30 doubles and 10 triples, and scored 100 runs. In the World Series against the Yankees, his grand-slam won Game 4 for St. Louis. In Game 7, he paced a 7-5 win with a single, double and home run. He was named the National League's Most Valuable Player.

One year later, he was gone from St. Louis. The team's seventh-place finish in 1965 led to wholesale changes. Boyer was traded to the New York Mets, where he spent parts of two seasons before joining the White Sox midway through 1967. In 1969, after a brief stay with the Dodgers, he retired at age 38.

In 1978, after managing in the minors for several years and coaching with the Cardinals for two, Boyer replaced Vern Rapp as the manager in St. Louis. The next year, he led the Cardinals to 86 wins and a third-place finish. But when the team got off to an 18-33 start in 1980, Boyer was fired and replaced by Whitey Herzog. The next fall, he was all set to manage the Cardinals' top farm club in Louisville when he was diagnosed with lung cancer. Ten months later, Boyer was dead at 51.

In 1984, the Cardinals retired Boyer's uniform number 14 in a ceremony at Busch Stadium. He was the fourth player so honored.

Busch Stadium
1965

At the end of 1965, stadium workers lowered the team's 1964 World Series banner. It had been a disappointing follow-up to their championship year. Although they scored the third highest number of runs in the National League and Bob Gibson won 20 games, the team struggled with injuries and finished in seventh place. However, it would be only two seasons before the Cardinals found themselves back on top.

Orlando Cepeda
First baseman, 1966 - 1968

Slugger Orlando Cepeda's short stay in St. Louis helped produce back-to-back National League pennants.

Cepeda came to St. Louis from the San Francisco Giants, where he'd been a six-time All Star and the 1958 NL Rookie of the Year. But he was traded to the Cardinals after a knee injury in 1965.

Cepeda dubbed his new team "El Birdos" and with his booming bat and fun-loving personality, he quickly became the centerpiece of the St. Louis offense. He took over first base from the departed Bill White and began delivering in key situations. Teammate Lou Brock called him "a great clutch hitter. He was at his best when the game was on the line." Cepeda followed his .303 average in

1966 with an even better showing the next year, when his .325 average and 111 RBIs were tops in the league. When the Cardinals won the NL title that season, he was named the league's Most Valuable Player

In the clubhouse, Cepeda kept the atmosphere loose by playing selections from his jazz collection on a booming stereo. But his average and power stats dropped dramatically in 1968 and at the end of the season, he was traded to Atlanta for Joe Torre.

Cepeda had his last big year in 1970. He finished his career as a designated hitter in the American League and retired after the 1974 season. In 1999, he was elected to the Hall of Fame.

Roger Maris
Outfielder, 1967 - 1968

Before he was traded to the Cardinals, Roger Maris was considering retirement. The two-time American League MVP was hounded by the press in New York before and after he broke Babe Ruth's home-run record by hitting 61 in 1961. He was portrayed as moody and uncooperative and nothing like his popular teammate, Mickey Mantle. Over time, nagging injuries to his hands and wrists robbed him of his power so that by 1966, he was miserable. But his trade to the Cardinals during the off-season provided a fresh start.

In St. Louis, Maris took over right field. His aggressive play and quiet, no-nonsense personality were appreciated by Cardinals fans. Although he never approached the power numbers of his early days with the Yankees, Maris was much happier playing in St. Louis. Finally rid of the media crush that comes with playing in New York, Maris also was closer to his family, who lived in Kansas City.

In the 1967 World Series, Maris batted .385 with a team-high seven RBI. When Maris again thought about retiring, team owner Gussie Busch promised him a Budweiser distributorship if he returned for another season. But injuries limited him to 100 games, many as a pinch-hitter. Finally, in 1968, the 34-year-old Maris left the game to tend to his new business in Gainesville, Florida, where he died of lymphoma in 1985.

Roger Maris and sons
Busch Stadium, 1967

During the middle of his first season in St. Louis, Roger Maris and his four sons posed for photographers before a game at Busch Stadium. Surrounding their dad are Kevin, Richard, Roger, Jr. and Randy. In 1998, the Maris family would return to Busch Stadium to watch another Cardinal, Mark McGwire, break Roger's single-season home-run record of 61.

Nelson Briles and Ray Washburn
Busch Stadium, 1968

The pitching staff drove the Cardinals to the 1968 National League title. With Bob Gibson setting the standard, St. Louis pitchers topped the league with a 2.49 ERA and 30 shut-outs. Right-handers Nellie Briles and Ray Washburn had the best year of their careers. Briles won 19 games and threw four shut-outs.

Washburn went 14-8 and threw a no-hitter against the Giants. It was the first no-hitter by a Cardinals pitcher in 27 years.

But neither man was successful in the World Series as the Tigers defeated the Cardinals in seven games.

Bob Gibson
1968

Bob Gibson's 1968 season will long be remembered as the most dominant pitching performance of the modern era.

It's not just that Gibson overpowered hitters to win 22 games. His 13 shut-outs and 268 strike-outs led the National League. During one stretch, he won 15 consecutive games, including a streak of 47 2/3 scoreless innings. His ERA of 1.12 was the lowest of the century by any pitcher with at least 300 innings. In honor of his stunning success, Gibson received the Cy Young Award and was named the league's Most Valuable Player.

In the World Series, Gibson threw three complete games and twice defeated Detroit's 30-game winner, Denny McLain. He struck out 17 and blanked the Tigers in Game 1. Four days later, he struck out 10 to win Game 4. His 35 strike-outs in 27 innings set a new World Series record. Unfortunately, his two victories for the Cardinals were offset by a Tigers win in Game 7, giving the title to Detroit.

1968 would long be remembered as the year of the pitcher. Gibson's success — along with that of McLain, Juan Marichal and others — would cause baseball to lower the height of the pitching mound the next year so that hitters would have a fighting chance. But Gibson would continue to dominate. He won 20 and 23 games each of the next two seasons and in 1971, he threw the only no-hitter of his distinguished career.

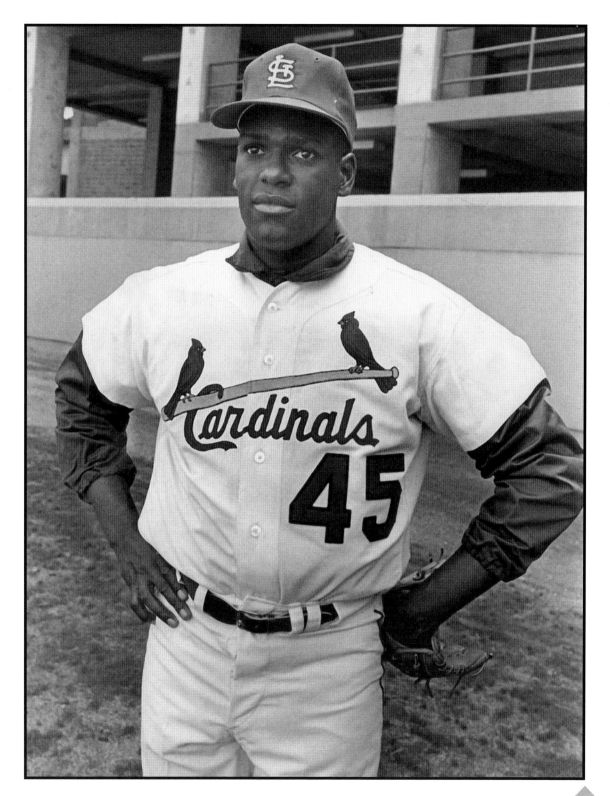

Roger Maris, Mike Shannon, Orlando Cepeda
World Series, 1968

The heart of the Cardinals' line-up couldn't secure a second straight championship for St. Louis. Despite two home runs by Cepeda and one by Shannon, the Cardinals lost the 1968 World Series to Detroit in seven games. Maris had only three hits, but scored five runs.

The next year, Cepeda and Maris would be gone and in 1970, Shannon's career would end prematurely because of illness. Cardinals fans would have to wait until 1982 to cheer another postseason appearance.

Lou Brock
World Series, 1968

Speedster Lou Brock was the lone bright spot for St. Louis in the World Series. His .464 average was the highest on either team and he also hit two home runs. On the base paths, Brock ran wild. He stole a record seven bases and scored six runs.

During most of his tenure in St. Louis, Brock was the National League's biggest thief. Starting in 1966, he led the league in steals for eight of the next nine seasons. The culmination of the streak was his record-shattering 118 steals in 1974. That year, Brock broke Maury Wills' major-league record of 102, set in 1962. Brock's record stood until Oakland's Rickey Henderson's got 130 in 1982.

Brock made a science of stealing bases, experimenting with the length of the leads he took off first base. He eventually settled on three and a half steps, allowing him to be in motion more quickly while avoiding being picked off. He characterized his style as "11 strides and a slide," and believed that speed alone wasn't the most important ingredient for stolen bases. Brock told *Sports Illustrated*, "The most important thing about base stealing is not stealing the base. It's disrupting the pitcher's concentration." Once on first base, with Cardinals fans chanting a chorus of "Lou, Lou," Brock was the game's most disruptive force.

By 1977, Brock had surpassed Ty Cobb as baseball's all-time stolen base king. When his career ended two years later, Brock's career total stood at 938. It would remain the game's all-time mark until Rickey Henderson surpassed it in 1991.

Red Schoendienst
Manager, 1965 - 1976, 1980

Red Schoendienst's 12 years at the helm remains the longest tenure for a Cardinals manager.

The front office turned to him when Johnny Keane suddenly resigned after the 1964 World Series. Schoendienst had served under Keane as a coach for two seasons and the easy-going former player was a popular choice among fans and players alike.

Schoendienst's first two seasons were difficult as the Cardinals struggled to play .500 ball. But the maturing of young players like Lou Brock and Julian Javier — along with the timely arrival of veterans Orlando Cepeda and Roger Maris — combined to take St. Louis to two straight titles.

But staying on top proved difficult. The Cardinals' farm system began failing to produce star players and several poor trades weakened the lineup. The team's 90 wins and second-place finish in 1971 was the high point of Schoendienst's last six years as manager. He was replaced after the 1976 season.

Schoendienst spent the next two years as a coach with the Oakland A's before rejoining the Cardinals in 1979. In 1980 and 1990, he briefly served as the team's interim manager. In 1989, he was elected to the Hall of Fame and in 1996, the Cardinals retired his uniform number 2.

Steve Carlton
Pitcher, 1965 - 1971

Steve Carlton won 329 games in the majors and recorded six seasons with 20 or more wins. Unfortunately for Cardinals fans, only one of those seasons came in St. Louis.

Carlton won 14 games in 1967, his first year in the Cardinals' starting rotation. Late that season, he flashed his potential by striking out 16 Phillies. Over the next two years, his blazing fastball and devastating curveball led to a 30-22 record. Against the Mets in September 1969, he set a record, since broken, by striking out 19 batters. His success led to berths on two consecutive All-Star teams.

But in the spring of 1970, Carlton and the front office tangled over salary. The negotiations got so heated that team owner Gussie Busch told the press, "I don't care if he throws another damn ball for us." By the time Carlton signed a two-year contract for $90,000, he had missed almost all of spring training. The late start affected his control and he struggled through a 10-19 season. The next year, he rebounded and with a 20-9 record, became the Cardinals' best pitcher. When it came time to sign another contract, he demanded to be paid like the league's other 20-game winners. He asked for $65,000. The Cardinals eventually countered with $60,000. When both sides refused to budge, Busch ordered Carlton traded to the Philadelphia Phillies for pitcher Rick Wise. It was the single worst deal in the club's history.

Carlton's first year in Philadelphia, he went 27-10 and led the National League in wins, ERA, complete games and strike-outs. Even more amazing is the fact that his success came on a last-place team that won only 57 games. As a result, Carlton was chosen as the National League's Cy Young Award winner. Over the next ten years, he was a four-time 20-game winner and collected another three Cy Young awards. When he retired in 1988, he was the second winningest left-hander of all time. Carlton was elected to the Hall of Fame in 1994.

Joe Torre
First and Third baseman, 1969 - 1974

When Joe Torre arrived in St. Louis from Atlanta, he immediately became the club's best run producer.

His first season, he led the team with 18 home runs and 101 RBI. His bat grew even stronger the next year when he averaged .325, collected 203 hits and knocked in another 100 runs. But the best was yet to come.

In 1971, Torre produced the greatest offensive year by a Cardinal since Stan Musial in 1948. He started the season with a 22-game hitting streak and at season's end, he led the National League with 230 hits, 137 RBI and a .363 average. He was named the league's Most Valuable Player.

Torre did all this while proving his versatility across the infield. A catcher in Atlanta, he replaced Cepeda at first base when he came to St. Louis. The next year, he briefly took over behind the plate when Tim McCarver was traded to the Phillies. And in 1971, he moved to third base when Mike Shannon was forced to retire.

The next three seasons saw Torre's numbers fall off and in 1974, he was traded to the New York Mets. There, he ended his playing career in 1977 and took over as manager for five losing seasons. In 1981, Torre began managing the Atlanta Braves, where he won a division title his first season. But he was fired in 1984 after two straight second-place finishes. He worked as a broadcaster for several years before returning to St. Louis in 1990 to manage the Cardinals.

Curt Flood
New York City, 1970

When the Cardinals traded Curt Flood to the Phillies after the 1969 season, he refused to report to Philadelphia. Flood asked Commissioner Bowie Kuhn to declare him a free agent. When his request was refused, he filed a lawsuit challenging baseball's reserve clause.

Flood, a 12-year veteran, believed he should have a say in where he played. His fight would prove a lonely one as not a single player testified on his behalf. In New York's Federal District Court, his lawyers argued that the game's arcane rules unfairly restricted players from selling their services on the open market. The case eventually found its way to the United States Supreme Court, which ruled in baseball's favor. But Flood's lawsuit led to other court challenges and by 1976, players were allowed to become free agents once their contracts expired. The explosion in player salaries over the next three decades is a direct result of Flood's courageous stand. But all the legal wrangling never benefited Flood.

Flood sat out the 1970 season and signed with the Washington Senators for the 1971 season. But he played in only 13 games before quitting and moving to Europe, where he spent the next five years. When he returned to the States in 1976, he spent one season broadcasting Oakland A's games, then ran a youth baseball program in the San Francisco Bay area. Flood died of throat cancer in 1997 at age 59.

Rick Wise
Pitcher, 1972 - 1973

The Cardinals traded Hall-of-Fame pitcher Steve Carlton to the Phillies for pitcher Rick Wise, who in 1971, had won 17 games and thrown a no-hitter for the last-place Phillies. But Wise's stay in St. Louis was brief.

His first year in St. Louis, the team's anemic offense limited him to a 16-16 record, despite a 3.11 ERA. The next April, the team got off to a pathetic 3-16 start, with Wise notching all three wins. He was chosen to be the starting pitcher in that summer's All-Star game, but over the second half of the season, he slumped and ended up 16-12, despite throwing five shut-outs.

The big right-hander was an excellent hitter. He hit 15 home runs during his career, including three for the Cardinals in 1973. But St. Louis needed more offense and so in 1974, the Cardinals traded him to the Boston Red Sox for outfielder Reggie Smith. Wise won a career-high 19 games for Boston in 1975 before spending another six years with Cleveland and San Diego.

Jose Cruz
Outfielder, 1970 - 1974

The best years for Jose Cruz came after he left St. Louis.

The slender outfielder patterned his swing after fellow Puerto Rican slugger Orlando Cepeda, but Cruz's big swing produced little power. While he struggled with the language, the Cardinals' front office grew impatient with his problems at the plate. In his two seasons as an everyday player, Cruz failed to hit above .235. When veteran Reggie Smith and rookie Bake McBride arrived in St. Louis, Cruz became expendable. He was sold to the Houston Astros for $25,000 after the 1974 season.

In Houston, Cruz became one of the greatest players in franchise history. He hit over .300 six times in 13 seasons and led the Astros in RBI seven times. He became a constant threat on the base paths, stealing 30 or more bases in five seasons. And in 1983, he led the National League with 189 hits.

Cruz was traded to the Yankees after the 1987 season and retired the next year. In 1997, he began coaching with the Astros.

Ken Reitz
Third baseman, 1972 - 1975; 1977 - 1980

The Zamboni machine is a hulking device used to sweep the ice at hockey arenas. It's also the name that Cardinals players gave the machine that swept the artificial turf at Busch Stadium. And it is the nickname that teammates gave Ken Reitz because of his brilliant glove work.

While Reitz was slow a foot, his quick reflexes and sure hands put him in the company of the era's finest third basemen. After leading the league in fielding percentage his first two years in St. Louis, Reitz won a Gold Glove in 1975.

The next year, St. Louis traded Reitz to San Francisco, where he spent a single season before returning to the Cardinals. Never more than an average batter, Reitz hit a career-high 17 home runs his first year back and continued to excel in the field. His nine errors were an all-time low for his position. Named team captain in 1978, he was selected to the All-Star team in 1980.

The arrival of manager Whitey Herzog brought an end to Reitz's time in St. Louis. Along with Leon Durham, he was traded to the Cubs for Bruce Sutter before the 1981 season. In Chicago, Reitz played so poorly that the Cubs released him after only one season. He spent a month with the Pirates in 1982 before his admitted drug use ended his career at age 30. Reitz attempted a comeback in the minors, but his dependency left him broke and out of work. He later returned to the St. Louis area to work as a chemical abuse counselor.

Al Hrabosky
Pitcher, 1970 - 1977

Famous for his intimidating scowl and bushy facial hair, Al Hrabosky became one of the game's most dominating closers.

Hrabosky captured the imagination of Cardinals fans midway through the 1974 season by creating an alter-ego dubbed "the Mad Hungarian." He stalked the mound with a menacing glare, slammed the ball into his glove and challenged hitters with his blazing fastball. His antics and ability to psych himself up between batters made him a fan favorite and marked the turning point in his career. When he was left off the 1974 All-Star team, the team hastily arranged an "Al Hrabosky Hbanner Hday" at Busch Stadium. The huge crowd hung hundreds of banners around the stadium to show support for Hrabosky.

In 1975, Hrabosky led the National League with 22 saves and was named Fireman of the Year by *The Sporting News*. But two years later, the hiring of manager Vern Rapp changed things. Rapp was a stern disciplinarian who instituted a policy banning facial hair. Hrabosky claimed his Fu Manchu mustache was critical to his success. He and Rapp feuded openly. The next season, the Mad Hungarian's act was playing in Kansas City. Two years later, he moved on to Atlanta, where arm problems ended his career in 1982.

Hrabosky later returned to St. Louis and joined the Cardinals' broadcast team.

Lou Brock, Bake McBride and Reggie Smith
1974

The Cardinals failed to win a division title during the 1970s, but placed second in 1971, 1973 and 1974. The success of the 1974 season was driven largely by the power hitting of the outfield trio. Brock, McBride and Smith all batted over .300, marking the first time since 1940 that the team's everyday outfielders bested .300 in the same season.

Reggie Smith had a superb year, hitting a team-high 23 home runs and a career-high 100 RBI. Lou Brock led the team with 194 hits and led the league with 118 stolen bases. Bake McBride batted .309 and stole 30 bases. Yet, the Cardinals finished 1½ games behind the Pittsburgh Pirates for the Eastern Division title.

Arnold "Bake" McBride
Outfielder, 1973 - 1977

Drafted by St. Louis in the 37th round, Bake McBride became the 1974 National League Rookie of the Year.

McBride tore through the minor leagues with his raw athleticism and joined the Cardinals in his fourth season of professional ball. Called up in late 1973, he averaged .302 in the final 40 games. The next spring, he became the club's everyday centerfielder.

In 1974, McBride hit .309 and stole 30 bases. He also excelled in the field, committing only four errors all season. Leg injuries slowed him down over the next two years, but he continued to bat over .300. In 1976, McBride made the All-Star team, although a knee injury would later cost him the second half of the season.

Meanwhile, friction was brewing in the clubhouse. McBride chafed under the strict rules of Cardinals manager Vern Rapp, who criticized him as a loafer and forced him to cut his mustache and sideburns. That June, the Cardinals traded McBride to the Phillies, where he helped win three division titles during five years with the team. In 1982, he was traded to the Cleveland Indians, where he was a reserve for two seasons before retiring in 1983 at age 34.

Mike Tyson
Infielder, 1972 - 1979

Mike Tyson's defensive skills got him to the major leagues, but his versatility kept him in St. Louis for seven full seasons.

His first three years with the Cardinals, Tyson played shortstop and in 1974, he led the league in double plays. Two years later, when veteran shortstop Don Kessinger arrived, Tyson was shifted to second base, where a series of injuries cost him half the season. Tyson's real value came in his ability to quickly execute the turn on double plays. Despite his mediocre performance at the plate, his quick release kept him in the Cardinals' lineup.

Tyson lost his everyday job to Ken Oberkfell in 1979 and when the season was over, he was traded to the Cubs. He retired two years later.

Ted Simmons
Catcher, 1968 - 1980

Fiery Ted Simmons was a rugged catcher and a powerful hitter whose leadership anchored the Cardinals' infield for more than a decade.

Drafted by St. Louis in the first round, Simmons took over behind the plate when Tim McCarver was traded to the Phillies in 1970. His long hair and powerful swing earned him the nickname "Simba," and he quickly earned a reputation as one of the game's best-hitting catchers.

In each of his first three seasons, Simmons, a switch-hitter, batted over .300. Soon, he became the Cardinals' leading run producer. Starting in 1972, he led the team in RBI for seven straight years. In addition, his 26 home runs in 1979 and his 96 RBI in 1972 remain the single-season record by a Cardinals' catcher.

Behind the plate, Simmons was the Cardinals' iron man, catching more than 150 games for seven straight seasons. A highlight came in 1971, when he caught Bob Gibson's no-hitter. Simmons' outspoken demeanor and his confident handling of the pitching staff made him the team's de facto leader. He didn't back down from a fight. He challenged opposing hitters, umpires and even his teammates with his candid assessments, some of which he delivered on his weekly radio show on KMOX during the off-season. He and fellow Cardinal Al Hrabosky entertained listeners with their lists of the game's "all-ugly" and "all hot-dog" teams.

In 1980, the Cardinals shook up their roster and traded Simmons to the Milwaukee Brewers as part of a seven-player deal. His five seasons with the Brewers included two straight division titles and a 1982 World Series appearance against the Cardinals. By 1983, Simmons was splitting time between catcher and first base and in 1986, he was traded to the Atlanta Braves, where he spent three final seasons as a reserve before retiring after the 1988 season.

Bob Gibson's retirement
1975

1974 marked Bob Gibson's final year in the Cardinals starting rotation. A series of knee and leg injuries had gradually robbed him of his effectiveness. Gibson's last big season was 1972, when he went 19-11.

The Cardinals honored Gibson before a sell-out crowd at Busch Stadium on September 1, 1975. Baseball Commissioner Bowie Kuhn presided over a ceremony that retired Gibson's uniform number. Accompanied by his mother, the 39-year-old star was given a bounty of gifts that included a 30-foot travel trailer.

Gibson remains the greatest pitcher in Cardinals history. He holds the record for wins, innings pitched, complete games, strike-outs and shut-outs. His 251 victories and 255 complete games will surely remain unchallenged.

John Denny
Pitcher, 1974 - 1979

John Denny's immense talent was overshadowed by his hair-trigger temper on the mound.

Denny was drafted out of high school in the 29th round and spent five unimpressive years in the minor leagues. But a strong showing during spring training in 1975 earned the 24-year-old a slot in the Cardinals' starting rotation. He won his first start and ended the season 10-7.

But Denny was a perfectionist who took offense when things didn't go his way. He barked at umpires, argued with coaches and blasted his teammates when misplays cost him a victory. His pitching coach in St. Louis, Claude Osteen, recalled, "He was in total chaos. He was his own worst enemy. Everything had to go absolutely perfect in order for him not to get upset. He lost so many ballgames because of that."

In his second season with St. Louis, Denny showcased his talent by winning the league's ERA crown. His 11 victories included three shut-outs. Only the Cardinals' anemic offense kept him from more wins. Typical of his outings that season was a game against the Cubs at Wrigley Field in August. With two outs in the eighth inning, Denny had a no-hitter going, but lost 2-1 in 10 innings.

In 1978, Denny's 14 wins led the staff as the Cardinals went 69-93 and finished fifth. But a sore arm limited him to eight wins the next season and he was traded to Cleveland for Bobby Bonds. Denny eventually landed in Philadelphia where in 1983, he had his greatest season. His 19 wins led the league and after the Phillies won the pennant, Denny was named the league's Cy Young Award winner. Denny credited his success to having become a Christian and mentoring by veteran Steve Carlton. His victory in Game 1 of the World Series was Philadelphia's only win against the Baltimore Orioles, who took the series in five games. Denny retired after the 1986 season.

Keith Hernandez
First baseman, 1974 - 1983

Keith Hernandez's stellar defense and 11 Gold Glove awards earned him a reputation as the finest-fielding first baseman of his era.

Hernandez came to St. Louis late in 1974 after winning a batting title in the minors with Tulsa. But he struggled at the plate and didn't become an everyday player until 1976. The next year, he batted .291 and hit three grand-slam home runs. But his greatest season came in 1979, when he won the National League batting title and was chosen the league's co-MVP along with Pittsburgh's Willie Stargell.

Hernandez's aggressive play at first base endeared him to Cardinals fans. He routinely charged bunts and threw to second to force an out. With his range and strong arm, he led the league's first basemen in assists five times and put-outs four times. He quickly became one of the team's leaders on and off the field, and was selected to five All-Star teams.

In 1980, Hernandez batted .321 and led the league in runs scored for the second straight year. Two years later, he helped lead the Cardinals to their first title in 18 years. He batted .299 and his 94 RBI were second highest on the team. In the World Series against the Milwaukee Brewers, he went hitless in the first four games, but knocked in eight runs in the final three games as St. Louis won the series in seven games.

Off the field, Hernandez faced distractions. His marriage was crumbling and rumors of drug use, later substantiated, began to circulate. In June 1983, he was suddenly traded to the Cardinals' hated rival, the New York Mets. St. Louis fans were outraged. In New York, Hernandez helped anchor a team that would win division titles in 1986 and 1988. His keen batting eye allowed Hernandez to lead the league in walks in 1987. His six-plus seasons as a Met were followed by one year in Cleveland in 1990, after which he retired.

Bob Forsch
Pitcher, 1974 - 1988

Bob Forsch was a 20-game winner and the only Cardinals pitcher to throw two no-hitters.

Forsch played third base when he was drafted by the Cardinals in 1968, but became a pitcher his third year in the minors. He proved a quick study, throwing no-hitters in 1972 and 1973. Halfway through the next season, he joined the Cardinals and went 7-4. The next year, he won 15 games and led the starting staff with a 2.86 ERA.

In 1977, Forsch won 20 games by baffling hitters with a superb curveball. His performance was even more remarkable considering he suffered from a bad lower back and notched his 20th win with his right thigh tightly wrapped.

Early the next season, Forsch threw the first no-hitter of his major-league career. It happened on April 15 before a sparse crowd of 11,495 at Busch Stadium. He threw only 96 pitches to blank the Phillies, 5-0.

Over the next four years, Forsch's record mirrored the Cardinals' up-and-down performance. In 1982, he went a staff-best 15-9 as the Cardinals won the National League pennant, but he lost both starts in the World Series against the Brewers.

His perfect form struck again in the final week of the 1983 season. On September 26, he no-hit the Montreal Expos and won, 3-0, at home.

Forsch won 14 games in 1986, his last big season in St. Louis. He ranks third on the Cardinals' all-time list for wins, strike-outs and innings pitched. Late in 1988, the 38-year-old was traded to the Houston Astros, where he spent one final season before retiring.

Ken Oberkfell
Infielder, 1977 - 1984

Ken Oberkfell's steady defensive play kept him in the majors for parts of 16 seasons. A shortstop in the minors, Oberkfell became a second baseman when the Cardinals slotted a prospect named Garry Templeton to play short. Oberkfell was a durable player who played through injuries and rarely missed a game. His lack of power at the plate was overlooked because of his stellar glove work. In five seasons with the Cardinals, Oberkfell never hit more than three home runs or knocked in more than 50 RBI a year. He was a line-drive hitter whose average consistently hovered near .300.

In 1981, Oberkfell changed positions again, moving to third base to make room for rookie second baseman Tommy Herr. The move worked and Oberkfell twice led the National League's third basemen in fielding average. But the Cardinals were desperate for pitching help and in 1984, they sent Oberkfell to Atlanta for lefty Ken Dayley. Oberkfell spent four seasons with the Braves before bouncing among four other teams during his last four years in the majors. He retired after the 1992 season.

Garry Templeton
Shortstop, 1976 - 1981

Garry Templeton's six seasons in St. Louis were marked by flair on the field and controversy off it.

Templeton was a gifted fielder with a knack for making the exceptional play. And he could hit. His first full season in St. Louis, the 21-year-old batted .322 with 200 hits. He led the National League in triples for three straight years. In 1979, he hit .314 and led the league with 211 hits. That season, the switch-hitter became the first player to collect 100 hits from both sides of the plate in the same season.

But behind the scenes, all was not well. In 1979, Templeton was upset when he wasn't chosen to start the All-Star Game and he refused to go as a reserve. He sparred with the front office over his contract and told reporters he might not give his all on the field. He told radio listeners that he no longer wanted to play for the Cardinals and demanded a trade. In 1980, he antagonized his teammates by sitting out a game, claiming he was too tired to play. After he pouted over being dropped from the lead-off spot, fans began to question his hustle on the field.

Things came to a head on August 26, 1981, during an afternoon game at Busch Stadium against the Giants. Templeton failed to run to first base when the third strike got by the catcher. Fans booed him as he returned to the dugout. Templeton made an obscene gesture before manager Whitey Herzog pulled him off the field. He was fined, suspended and treated for depression before ultimately being sent packing. Templeton was traded to San Diego for shortstop Ozzie Smith when the season ended. The trade brought the Cardinals a franchise player destined for the Hall of Fame.

In San Diego, Templeton continued to wow onlookers with his spectacular defense, but he was never the offensive force he had been in St. Louis. In 10 seasons with the Padres, Templeton hit above .270 only once and collected more than 140 hits only once. He retired after the 1991 season.

Lou Brock's 3,000th hit
Busch Stadium, 1979

At 39, Lou Brock was determined to close his career on a high note after finishing a sub-par 1978 with 2,900 career hits.

By mid-July, Brock was hitting .320 and leading the league in batting. On August 13, before more than 46,000 cheering fans at home, Brock collected his 3,000th hit off Chicago Cubs pitcher Dennis Lamp. On hand to congratulate

Brock were team owner Augie Busch and Hall-of-Famer Stan Musial.

Brock also collected his 938th career stolen base that season, temporarily moving him into first place on baseball's all-time list. He retired with a .293 career average and the Cardinals retired his uniform number 20 that year. Brock was inducted into the Hall of Fame in 1985.

**Willie Stargell and Keith Hernandez
1980**

In 1979, Keith Hernandez had the best season of his career. He hit .344 to win the National League batting title and lead the league in runs scored, doubles and on-base percentage. He produced a career-high 105 RBI and his 210 hits fell only one behind teammate Garry Templeton for tops in the league. For his efforts, Hernandez was chosen the league's co-MVP along with the Pirates' Willie Stargell. The next season, the two picked up their awards and posed for photographers at Busch Stadium. At 39, Stargell had led Pittsburgh to a World Series title in his final season as an everyday player. It is the only time in major league history that two players shared the award.

George Hendrick
Outfielder, 1978 - 1984

George Hendrick's booming bat generated a steady power source during his playing days with the Cardinals.

After arriving from San Diego in early 1978, the eight-year veteran batted over .300 three times and produced the only two 100-plus RBI seasons of his career. Nicknamed "Silent George" for his refusal to talk to the media, Hendrick was loved by teammates and fans. In 1980, he had the greatest year of his career, hitting .302 and leading the team with 25 home runs and 109 RBI.

When the Cardinals won the National League pennant in 1982, Hendrick's 19 home runs and 104 RBI led the way. In the World Series against Milwaukee, he batted .321 with five RBI and his game-winning hit in Game 7 gave St. Louis the championship. After the 1984 season, the Cardinals, desperate for starting pitching, traded Hendricks to Pittsburgh for John Tudor. Hendricks spent his last three years with the California Angels before retiring after the 1988 season.

Dane Iorg
Outfielder, 1977 - 1984

Terry "Tito" Landrum
Outfielder, 1980 - 1987

Once he reached the major leagues, Dane Iorg, an All-American at Brigham Young University, became the Cardinals' most valuable reserve.

Although he hit for a high average, Iorg had almost no power and hit only 14 home runs in 10 major-league seasons. He did, however, have a knack for getting clutch hits. In 1980, he batted .303 with 23 doubles, and in one game against Atlanta, he drove in seven runs. The next year, he led the National League in batting with runners in scoring position. In the 1982 World Series, he became the club's designated hitter and produced a .529 average and four doubles.

Iorg was traded to the Kansas City Royals early in 1984 and came back to haunt St. Louis in the 1985 World Series. Iorg's two-run pinch-hit single in the bottom of the ninth won Game 6 for the Royals, who finished off the Cardinals the next night to win the series. Iorg finished his career with San Diego in 1986.

Tito Landrum spent eight long years in the minors and nine years in the majors on the bench.

Landrum was unable to crack the Cardinals' everyday outfield, which included more talented players such as Lonnie Smith, Willie McGee and Vince Coleman. In 1983, Landrum spent part of the season with Baltimore, where he hit a home run to win Game 3 of the American League Championship Series and send the Orioles to the World Series. He returned to the Cardinals in 1984, where his speed and athleticism made him a valuable bench player. He became the team's primary pinch-hitter for the next two seasons.

When Vince Coleman went down prior to Game 4 of the 1985 National League Championship Series, Landrum was there to pick up the slack. He had four hits and three RBI in the final three games of the series. In the World Series against Kansas City, Landrum played all seven games and hit a team-high .360. He and the Royals' Willie Wilson were the only two players to hit safely in all seven games. Traded to the Dodgers in 1987, Landrum finished up with Baltimore in 1988.

Tommy Herr
Second baseman, 1979 - 1988

Tommy Herr was a critical component of the Cardinals' three National League titles during the 1980s, but on a team of marquee players, his steady play often was overlooked.

Manager Whitey Herzog thought so much of Herr that he shifted second baseman Ken Oberkfell to third base in 1981 to make room for the rookie. Herr led the league's second basemen in fielding percentage his first season as an everyday player. And during his seven years in St. Louis, he and shortstop Ozzie Smith led the league in double plays three times.

Never a big power hitter, the switch-hitter excelled at running the bases when Cardinals sluggers came to bat. He stole more than 20 bases in 1981 and 1982. Knowledgeable fans knew the gritty Herr, who battled through three knee operations, was the heart and soul of their championship teams. Herzog called him "the guts of the team." In 1985, when the Cardinals again won the NL pennant, Herr made the All-Star team and had the best year of his career. He batted .302, stole 31 bases and collected a team-high 110 RBI. It was only the seventh time in league history that a second baseman knocked in more than 100 runs in a season. In the pennant-clinching series against the Dodgers, he had four doubles and six RBI.

Early in 1988, fans were shocked when the Cardinals traded Herr to their World Series opponent, the Minnesota Twins. Herr spent just one season with the Twins before being traded to the Phillies. He also played with the Mets and Giants before retiring after the 1991 season.

Whitey Herzog
Manager, 1980 - 1990

Whitey Herzog managed the Cardinals during the second greatest decade in franchise history, transforming the team into a perennial contender.

When he arrived from Kansas City in 1980, the team was in disarray and hadn't won anything since 1968. Given complete authority by owner Gussie Busch, Herzog set out to rebuild the Cardinals around pitching and defense. The cavernous dimensions of Busch Stadium limited home runs, so he assembled a lineup that showcased the team's speed. During the 1980 winter meetings, he was a blur of activity, swapping players almost every day. He solved the team's bullpen problems by acquiring a proven closer, Bruce Sutter, from the Cubs. A year later, he stole minor-leaguer Willie McGee from the Yankees, outfielder Lonnie Smith from the Phillies and pitcher Joaquin Andujar from the Astros. The final piece fell into place when he sent the disgruntled Garry Templeton to San Diego for shortstop Ozzie Smith. Herzog's success quickly became evident: three National League pennants and one World Series title in the next six years. His style of baseball was dubbed "Whitey ball" and twice he was named baseball's Executive of the Year.

Herzog's outspoken, no-nonsense approach thrived in part because of his relationship with Busch, who gave his manager total authority because he spent the team's money wisely and produced results. Herzog summed up their relationship in his book, *The White Rat*, saying, "One man in charge. No committees. No crap."

In 1982, the Cardinals won 92 games, their best showing in 14 years and attendance doubled. In 1985, the club's 101 victories marked the second time since 1944 that it surpassed the 100-win mark. When the Cardinals won a third NL title in 1987, the team drew more than three million fans for the first time ever. But Busch's death in 1989 ushered in a new era. The brewery stopped bankrolling the signing of free agents and the team's general manager, Dal Maxvill, couldn't duplicate Herzog's penchant for making deals. With the team in sixth place early in 1990, Herzog resigned and was replaced by Joe Torre.

Herzog worked briefly in the front office of the California Angels before writing a second book in the 1990s on his objections to the way the game was played on and off the field.

Darrell Porter
Catcher, 1981 - 1985

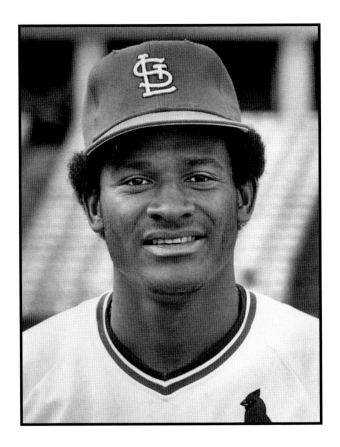

David Green
Outfielder, 1981 - 1984; 1987

Veteran catcher Darrell Porter faced two big issues when he arrived in St. Louis.

First, in Kansas City, where he had played for Whitey Herzog, Porter admitted to a decade of drug and alcohol abuse. After undergoing treatment, he came to St. Louis as a free agent, but Herzog raised eyebrows by giving him a $3.5 million, five-year contract. Second, his arrival meant catcher and fan favorite Ted Simmons would be traded, leading Cardinals fans to think Herzog had lost his mind. Yes, Porter was a superb defensive catcher, but even Herzog had to know that Porter couldn't replace Simmons' powerful bat.

Complicating matters, Porter got off to a slow start in St. Louis. A torn rotator cuff cost him most of 1981 and he started 1982 with a broken hand. When he hit .231 with 12 home runs and 48 RBI that season, Cardinals fans were livid. But surprisingly, Porter became the hero of the 1982 postseason. In the National League Championship Series against Atlanta, he was on base constantly. He walked five times and had five hits, including three doubles, to help the Cardinals sweep the Braves. In the World Series against Milwaukee, his eight hits drove in five runs and helped lead St. Louis to the title. Porter was named the MVP of the NLCS and the World Series.

But by 1985, injuries kept him from catching every day. When the season ended, Porter signed with the Texas Rangers as a free agent. He retired two years later.

David Green was a top prospect whose off-field problems kept him from realizing his major-league potential.

Green came to the Cardinals in the seven-player deal that sent Ted Simmons to Milwaukee. Some saw him as the next Roberto Clemente because of his speed, power and strong arm. Green liked the comparison and modeled his game after the Puerto Rican star. In 1983, he hit .284 with 10 triples and 34 stolen bases.

But his success was hampered by problems off the field. Green came from Nicaragua, where civil war was tearing apart the country. His brother was imprisoned and Green fought to bring his mother to the United States. She arrived in late 1983, but died that winter. Green began drinking and his game deteriorated. Shifted to first base, he hit a career-high 15 home runs in 1984, but struck out 105 times. When the season ended, he was traded to the Giants, along with two other players, for slugger Jack Clark. Over the next three years, Green played in the Mexican and Japanese leagues before getting a final brief shot with St. Louis late in 1987.

Joaquin Andujar
Pitcher, 1981 - 1985

Joaquin Andujar was a two-time 20-game winner for St. Louis whose flamboyant personality kept him in the headlines.

Andujar arrived in St. Louis midway through the strike-shortened 1981 season and went 6-1 down the stretch, including a streak of 21 scoreless innings. The next year, he won 15 games and led the staff in ERA, complete games, strike-outs and fewest walks. But he was at his best in the postseason, where he won Game 3 of the National League Championship Series against Atlanta and dominated Milwaukee batters in the World Series. He won Games 3 and 7, and had an ERA of 1.35 for the series.

The next year, Andujar struggled. He went 6-16, although many losses could be blamed on pathetic run support. In eight of those games, the Cardinals scored a total of four runs. The hot-tempered pitcher would show his frustration with the mounting losses, sometimes by trashing a portion of the locker room. Still, he prospered under Whitey Herzog and finally, in 1984, he won a league-best 20 games, including four shut-outs. For good measure, he hit two home runs, including a grand-slam against the Braves.

Andujar was proud of his Dominican heritage and sensitive to criticism from fans or sportswriters. He dubbed himself "one tough Dominican" and proclaimed his keys to success: "I just say two things. Work hard, keep your head up and screw it." His favorite all-purpose expression was "youneverknow."

In 1985, Andujar started the season on a tear. In his first 23 starts, he went 17-4 with a 2.31 ERA. But when he wasn't chosen to start the All-Star Game, Andujar refused to attend. He ended the season 21-12, but pitched poorly in both of his NLCS starts against the Dodgers, allowing 10 runs in just over 10 innings.

Andujar left his most lasting impression in the World Series against the Royals. Although he lost Game 3, he was called upon to relieve in Game 7 with the Cardinals trailing, 10-0. But he allowed umpire Don Denkinger's ball and strike calls to unnerve him, and charged off the mound in a frenzy on national TV. When order finally was restored, both Andujar and Whitey Herzog were ejected from the game and the Cardinals were finished. Andujar was suspended for 10 days. Later, he was traded to Oakland, where he retired two years later.

Bruce Sutter
Pitcher, 1981 - 1984

Bruce Sutter solved the Cardinals' most pressing need: a reliever who could be counted on to close a game. The year before he came to town, the bullpen had blown 22 late-inning leads.

In Chicago, Sutter was the National League's most dominant closer. Relying almost exclusively on his split-finger fastball, he led the league in saves for two straight years and won the 1979 Cy Young Award. But when he was awarded a $700,000 salary in arbitration, the Cubs' ownership was outraged and traded him to St. Louis for third baseman Ken Reitz, first baseman Leon Durham and a minor-leaguer. The move demonstrated that Cardinals manager Whitey Herzog was serious about building a winner.

His first year in St. Louis, Sutter led the league with 25 saves. Overall, the Cardinals had the best record in the National League's Eastern Division and only the split season, due to a players' strike, kept them out of the playoffs. In 1982, Sutter notched 36 saves as the Cardinals won the division and the World Series. He was on the mound for the last two innings of Game 7 to secure the championship for St. Louis. His performance earned him *The Sporting News*' Fireman of the Year award for the second straight year. In 1983, Sutter suffered control problems and managed only 21 saves, but the next year he corrected a flaw in his delivery and roared back with 45 saves to tie the major league single-season mark.

Sutter's success made him highly attractive to other teams. When his contract ended after the 1984 season, he was lured away by the Atlanta Braves. He signed the then-richest pitching contract in baseball history by inking a six-year $10 million deal. But Sutter had only one good year for the Braves. After 23 saves in 1985, he suffered a torn rotator cuff and missed almost two full seasons. Three shoulder operations later, he returned in 1988, but the magic was gone. He retired prior to the 1989 season with 300 career saves, then the all-time mark for a reliever in the majors.

Willie McGee
Outfielder, 1982 - 1990; 1996 - 1999

Willie McGee's dazzling talent and humble demeanor made him a fan favorite for more than a decade. His blazing speed and ability to get on base defined the type of player Whitey Herzog wanted at Busch Stadium.

St. Louis spotted McGee playing in the Yankees' minor-league system where in 1981, he batted .322 with 20 doubles and 24 stolen bases in only 100 games. The Cardinals gave up pitcher Bob Sykes to get McGee. It turned out to be the most lopsided deal for St. Louis since acquiring Lou Brock almost 20 years earlier.

McGee started in Louisville, but injuries to George Hendrick and David Green opened the door to the rookie outfielder. His first year, he batted .296 and stole 24 bases. His strong throwing arm and flare for sensational catches landed him the job in centerfield. When the Cardinals made the postseason, McGee was at his best. In the National League Championship Series against Atlanta, he batted .308 and drove in five runs as St. Louis won three straight games. In Game 3 of the World Series, McGee hit two home runs and robbed the Brewers of two by bringing balls back into the park. In 1983, he made the All-Star team and won his first Gold Glove award.

McGee's finest season came in 1985, when with a .353 average, he became the second switch-hitter ever to win the NL batting crown. Over the next four years, hamstring injuries and knee surgery reduced his speed, but McGee remained a potent threat at the plate. In 1987, he drove in a career-high 105 runs and made his third All-Star team. That postseason, McGee batted .340 and drove in six runs.

By 1990, the Cardinals were struggling and the team was interested in developing young outfielders like Ray Lankford. And so, at the trading deadline, the Cardinals sent McGee to Oakland, where his .335 average made him the first player to win a batting title in one league after being traded from the other. McGee spent four years with the Giants and one with the Red Sox before returning to St. Louis in 1996, where he received a hero's welcome. His final four years were split between the outfield and the role of pinch-hitter. He retired after the 1999 season with 2,254 hits.

Ozzie Smith
Shortstop, 1982 - 1996

Ozzie Smith is the greatest defensive shortstop in major league history. It can be argued that he is the first player elected to the Hall of Fame strictly because of his defense.

Smith's jaw-dropping showmanship during his 19-year major-league career set a new standard for shortstops. He treated fans to fielding feats that defied description and his exceptional range allowed him to turn base hits into sure outs.

But his success was anything but certain. Growing up poor in the Watts section of Los Angeles, Smith's skills were self-taught. As a youngster, he spent countless hours lying on the floor of his room, tossing a baseball up in the air until he could repeatedly catch it with his eyes closed. The drill allowed Smith to develop a unique feel for the ball, but he couldn't do anything about his small size. He was not drafted out of high school and intent on getting an education, he attended Cal-Poly at San Luis Obispo.

In 1977, Smith was chosen by the San Diego Padres in the fourth round. He played only 68 games in Class A ball before the Padres made him their everyday shortstop in 1978. Smith's .258 average and 40 stolen bases placed him second in the balloting for Rookie of the Year honors. Over the next three seasons, he struggled at the plate, but wowed onlookers with his brilliant glove work, earning two Gold Gloves and making the All-Star team in 1980. He also picked up the nickname, "The Wizard of Oz." However, Smith and the Padres sparred repeatedly over money and after the 1981 season, he was traded to the Cardinals for disgruntled Garry Templeton. It proved a turning point for Smith and the fortunes of the Cardinals' franchise.

Smith's arrival coincided with the Cardinals 1982 championship season. It also began a 15-year love affair with fans, who quickly made him the most popular athlete in St. Louis. His nightly highlight-reel performances had fans coming to the stadium just to see him play. It was some show.

Lonnie Smith
Outfielder, 1982 - 1985

Lonnie Smith's powerful bat led him to four World Series appearances, but problems with consistency kept him bouncing around baseball.

Whitey Herzog acquired Smith from the Phillies after the 1981 season because of his bat and his speed. Despite a tendency to misplay balls in the outfield, which earned him the nickname "Skates," Smith proved to be a catalyst for the Cardinals offense. In 1982, he hit .307, stole 68 bases and led the league in runs scored. He finished second in the league's MVP balloting and helped propel the Cardinals to the World Series against the Milwaukee Brewers. There, he hit four doubles, a triple and scored six runs, while batting .321.

The next year, Smith briefly left the team in mid-season to undergo drug treatment. Finally sober, he returned to the lineup and ended the season with a .321 average and 43 steals. But in 1984, Smith was distracted by the death of his father and step-grandmother. His numbers slipped and his playing time diminished. When rookie speedster Vince Coleman arrived in 1985, Smith was traded to Kansas City. He spent only one season as an everyday player with the Royals, but managed to play in his third World Series and help defeat his former team before being released after the 1987 season.

Unable to find a major league team that wanted him, Smith was forced to go back to the minors in 1988. He signed with the Richmond Braves and quietly fought his way back to the majors. The next year, he was in Atlanta, where he put together the best year of his career. Despite playing for a team that lost 97 games and finished last, Smith's .315 batting average was third highest in the league. When the Braves won the 1991 NL pennant, Smith was in left field for his fourth World Series. He later spent time with Pittsburgh and Baltimore before retiring in 1994.

Jack Buck
Broadcaster, 1954 - 1959; 1961 - 2001

Jack Buck spent nearly 50 years behind the microphone as the voice of Cardinals baseball. He perfected his craft during four seasons in the Cardinals minor-league system before joining veteran announcer Harry Caray and former player Joe Garagiola in St. Louis in 1954. The trio lasted until 1959, when Buck was fired to make room for the return of Buddy Blattner. Buck spent a single season doing ABC's *Game of the Week*, where he announced the first game of the new American Football League, before rejoining Caray the next year. The duo spent another nine seasons together until Caray left for Oakland.

Out from under Caray's shadow, Buck developed his own thoughtful style and a new generation of Cardinals fans grew to appreciate his articulate, candid comments. Buck was joined by Mike Shannon in 1972 and for the next 30 years, the pair spread the Cardinals' gospel across the Midwest over KMOX's booming signal. Buck's low-key delivery was offset by Shannon's mangled analogies and head-scratching remarks. Health problems eventually forced Buck to cut back his schedule and 2001 was his last season behind the mike. His death the next June, at age 77, left three generations of Cardinals fans mourning the only announcer they'd ever known.

Gussie Busch
World Series, 1982

During the 1980s, there was no more colorful symbol of the Cardinals on-field success than owner Gussie Busch. Wearing his flaming red suit and matching cowboy hat, Busch would supervise the cheers from his box near the Cardinals' dugout. Before postseason games, he would circle the field onboard the Budweiser beer wagon, drawn by the brewery's world-famous team of Clydesdales. It created a grand spectacle and helped mark the team's almost constant success.

Tommy Herr, Keith Hernandez, Ozzie Smith and Ken Oberkfell
Busch Stadium, 1983

In 1982, the Cardinals' starting infield led the National League in fielding percentage and helped guide St. Louis to its first championship in 18 years. Hernandez led all first basemen in total put-outs and Smith led in assists. Both Smith and Oberkfell were tops in fielding at their respective positions.

At the time this photo was taken, the foursome's time together was almost over. Hernandez would be traded to the Mets in June. The next year, Oberkfell was shipped to Atlanta. Herr and Smith would soon be joined by Terry Pendleton and Jack Clark as the Cardinals returned to the World Series in 1985 and 1987.

Andy Van Slyke
Outfielder, 1983 - 1986

Versatile Andy Van Slyke was the Cardinals' first-round pick in the 1979 draft. Called up to St. Louis midway through the 1983 season, he made an immediate impression by hitting three home runs in his first 10 at-bats, all against the Cardinals' chief rival, the New York Mets. His .262 average, 15 doubles and 21 stolen bases in half a season landed him the Cardinals' Rookie of the Year award. Reporters and fans loved "Slick," as he was known, for his quick wit and amusing one-liners.

In 1984, Van Slyke drew 63 walks, stole 28 bases and had the second highest on-base percentage of the starting nine. Although he continued to play several positions, the Cardinals decided to take advantage of his strong arm by permanently positioning him in right field. There, word quickly spread that base runners better not test his arm.

In 1985, Van Slyke hit 13 home runs, the second highest total on the team. But Whitey Herzog grew impatient with him and rarely let him face left-handed pitchers. Despite leading the team in home runs and RBI in 1986, Van Slyke was dealt to the Pittsburgh Pirates in a trade that brought veteran catcher Tony Pena to the Cardinals. Allowed to play every day for the lowly Pirates, Van Slyke blossomed into one of the league's premier centerfielders. In 1987, he batted .293 with 36 doubles, 21 home runs and 34 stolen bases. The next year was even better. Van Slyke's 15 triples led the league and he had a career-high 21 home runs and 100 RBI. Beginning in 1990, Van Slyke helped lead the Pirates to three straight division titles and in 1992, he led the league in hits and doubles. After eight years in Pittsburgh, Van Slyke spent one final season as a reserve with the Orioles and Phillies before retiring after the 1995 season.

Terry Pendleton
Third baseman, 1984 - 1990

Terry Pendleton was a superb defensive third baseman whose best years came after he left St. Louis. Still, he gave the Cardinals their most gifted third baseman since Ken Boyer.

Like Boyer, Pendleton had great range, quick reflexes and a strong, accurate arm. While not blessed with the blazing speed of his teammates, Pendleton twice stole more than 20 bases in a season. His aggressive play and hard-nosed attitude also made him a leader in the clubhouse. Over time, he developed a reputation as one of the club's most dependable clutch hitters.

In 1987, Pendleton had his best year as a Cardinal. He hit .286 and won his first Gold Glove award. In addition, his 96 RBI were the most by a St. Louis third baseman since Joe Torre in 1971. But Pendleton's all-out style took its toll on his body. Playing on the harsh Astroturf surface at Busch Stadium left him with frequent knee and hamstring injuries, and cost him two months of the 1988 season. But he never gave up. In 1989, Pendleton won his second Gold Glove award.

Injuries and a .230 batting average in 1990 made Pendleton expendable. That off-season, he signed with the Atlanta Braves as a free agent and helped lead the resurgence of the franchise. His veteran leadership and a career year at the plate helped propel the Braves to the World Series. Pendleton won the National League batting title with a .319 average and his 187 hits were tops in the league. His efforts got him named the league's Most Valuable Player. In 1992, Pendleton made his first All-Star team and had the best year of his career. He hit 21 home runs and drove in 105 runners, while batting .311 and again leading the league in hits.

In 1995, Pendleton signed with the Florida Marlins, where he spent two seasons before finishing up with the Reds and Royals. He retired after the 1998 season.

Danny Cox
Pitcher, 1983 - 1988

Danny Cox's promising major league career was cut short by injuries.

Cox was a big, strong right-hander with a nasty curveball who rose quickly through the minor league ranks. In 1983, while pitching for Louisville, he was chosen to start the annual Hall of Fame exhibition game in Cooperstown. When he defeated the soon-to-be World Champion Baltimore Orioles, 4-1, the Cardinals promoted him to the majors. In his first start, he squared off against Steve Carlton of the Phillies, but lost, 1-0, in 11 innings. In his next start, he defeated Nolan Ryan and the Houston Astros, 5-2.

In 1984, Cox split time between the majors and the minors, winning nine games and throwing a three-hit shut-out against the Expos. The next year, he emerged as the Cardinals' number three starter, winning 18 games and putting together a stretch of 23 scoreless innings. He threw a pair of two hitters and narrowly missed a perfect game in May when he faced only 29 Reds before allowing a single in the eighth inning to Davey Concepcion. In the National League Championship Series against the Dodgers, Cox was the Cardinals' stopper as he won Game 3 after Los Angeles had taken the first two games. In the World Series, he posted a 1.80 ERA, but the Cardinals eventually lost to the Royals in seven games.

Cox's success was short-lived. During spring training in 1986, he chipped a bone in his ankle and finished the season with a 12-13 record. In 1987, he was 8-3 in early July when a line drive broke a bone in his right foot, disabling him for a month. When he returned, he went 3-6 over the rest of the season. He did, however, lock up the pennant against the Giants by shutting out San Francisco, 6-0, in Game 7 of the NLCS to send St. Louis to the World Series against the Minnesota Twins. Cox lost Game 2 but won Game 5 as the Twins took the series in seven games.

Arm problems in 1988 limited Cox to a 3-8 record and elbow surgery cost him the next two seasons. Released by St. Louis, Cox signed with the Phillies in 1991, but was never the same. He became a reliever, then spent five years with three different teams before retiring after the 1995 season.

Vince Coleman
Outfielder, 1985 - 1990

Vince Coleman is the only player to steal more than 100 bases in each of his first three seasons in the majors. Not even Lou Brock or Rickey Henderson can claim such a streak.

On a team powered by speed, Coleman's game was high octane. His first year in St. Louis, he set baseball's all-time rookie record with 110 steals, a total that equaled more than the combined efforts of 13 major league teams.

Coleman could also play defense. In the field, he displayed a strong, accurate throwing arm and his 16 outfield assists were second highest in the league. He was the unanimous choice to be the 1985 National League Rookie of the Year.

The next year, Coleman picked up where he left off. His 107 stolen bases included 15 games where he stole second and third base in the same inning.

When he swiped another 109 bases the next season, he ranked second on the Cardinals' all-time steal list after just three years. Over the next three seasons, Coleman led the league in steals, but his 81 thefts in 1988 marked the high point for the remainder of his career. Although Coleman came to steal less, he became more proficient at it. In 1989, he set the major league record by swiping 51 consecutive bases without being caught.

After the 1990 season, Coleman was allowed to sign with the New York Mets as a free agent. He played another seven years in the majors, but injuries slowed him down and he was never again an everyday player. He retired in 1997.

Ozzie Smith

During his 15 years with St. Louis, Ozzie Smith hit more than three home runs only once. But in 1985, he hit one of the most famous home runs in Cardinals history.

It happened in the National League Championship Series against the Los Angeles Dodgers, before a raucous crowd at Busch Stadium with the series tied at two wins apiece. With the game knotted 2-2 in the ninth inning, Smith came to the plate against Dodgers reliever Tom Niedenfuer. Smith got behind in the count, 1-2, but stroked the next pitch over the right field wall to win the game. Broadcaster Jack Buck urged listeners, "Go crazy, folks! Go crazy!" As Smith circled the bases with his right arm in the air, Cardinals fans erupted in a sea of sound. It was a most unlikely result from a most unexpected source and helped propel the Cardinals back to the World Series.

Jack Clark
First baseman, 1985 - 1987

Lacking a power hitter, the Cardinals long relied on the hit-and-run and the stolen base to score runs. But the arrival of slugger Jack Clark in 1985 changed that strategy with his immediate burst of power.

During his previous eight years with the San Francisco Giants, Clark had been among the National League's most dependable run producers. Despite being hampered by injuries and playing in wind-blown Candlestick Park, Clark had hit more than 20 home runs five times. In 1982, he also knocked in 103 runs, the fifth-highest total in the league.

Although his stay in St. Louis proved too short, Clark's impact was immediate. In his first at bat, he hit a home run against the Mets' Doc Gooden. A pulled rib cage muscle limited him to 126 games, but by season's end, Clark had hit 21 home runs and driven in 87 runs to lead the Cardinals to the postseason. In the National League Championship Series against the Dodgers, Clark hit one of the most dramatic home runs in team history. Facing Dodgers reliever Tom Niedenfuer in the top of the ninth inning of Game 6, with the Cardinals down to their final out and trailing, 5-4, "Jack the Ripper" hit a three-run home run to win the game and send St. Louis to the 1985 World Series.

But Clark couldn't seem to stay healthy. In June 1986, he hurt his thumb sliding into third base and was out for the season. Without him, the Cardinals slumped to a losing record and a third-place finish. When he returned in 1987, Clark had his best year ever. He hit 35 home runs and produced 106 RBI despite leading the league in walks. But the Cardinals' postseason aspirations were dealt a fatal blow when Clark went down with an ankle injury in September. His absence in the World Series proved crucial as the Cardinals lost the series to the Minnesota Twins in seven games.

As a free agent, Clark was unable to come to terms with the Cardinals' front office and so he signed with the Yankees for the 1988 season. His departure crippled the Cardinals offense, leaving the team without a bona fide power source until Mark McGwire arrived a decade later. Clark left New York and played two seasons each with the Padres and Red Sox before retiring after the 1992 season.

John Tudor
Pitcher, 1985 - 1988; 1990

Lefty John Tudor spent five years with the Red Sox and one with the Pirates before being traded to the Cardinals for outfielder George Hendrick. When he got off to a miserable 1-7 start in 1985, Cardinals fans were sure the deal was a dud. But things changed dramatically when a former high school teammate saw him pitch on television. The friend, who'd been his catcher in high school, noticed a flaw in his delivery and brought it to his attention. The result was immediate. Tudor began throwing with finesse and frustrating batters with pinpoint control. He reeled off 20 victories in his final 21 decisions. His 10 shutouts led the National League and his 1.93 ERA was second lowest in the league.

Tudor was at his best when the season was on the line. On September 11, Tudor held New York to three hits and beat Mets phenom Dwight Gooden, 1-0, in 10 innings to put the Cardinals in a first-place tie with New York. When St.

Louis won the pennant and moved on to the World Series, Tudor won Game 5 by shutting out the Royals. But he was roughed up in Game 7 and lasted less than three innings. When the moody pitcher entered the clubhouse, he punched an electrical fan and severely cut his hand.

Tudor pitched well in 1986 and won 13 games, but his 1987 season was interrupted by a freak accident. He broke a bone in his right leg when Mets catcher Barry Lyons fell on him while trying to catch a foul ball that drifted into the Cardinals dugout. Tudor missed more than three months before finishing the season with a 10-2 record. Arm problems in 1988 got him traded to the Dodgers, where he missed almost the entire 1989 season. He returned to St. Louis in 1990, where he won 12 games before retiring.

Jose Oquendo
Infielder, 1986 - 1995

For 10 years, Jose Oquendo was the Cardinals' super substitute. His ability to play any position earned him the nickname "Secret Weapon." In 1988, he caught — and pitched — an inning of relief to become the first National League player in 70 years to play all nine positions in a single season. He was such a gifted pinch-hitter that manager Whitey Herzog was reluctant to put him into the everyday lineup.

But the trade of Tommy Herr in 1988 opened the way for Oquendo to become the regular second baseman for two-plus seasons. Starting in 1989, he led the league's second basemen in fielding percentage for two straight years. He also worked on his hitting and in 1989, batted .291 with a 23-game hitting streak. But in 1992, he returned to a back-up role and spent another four years filling in where needed. He retired after the 1995 season, then spent a year managing in the minors. In 1999, he became the Cardinals' third-base coach.

Todd Worrell
Pitcher, 1985 - 1989; 1992

Todd Worrell, the 1986 National League Rookie of the Year, was a starting pitcher in the minors, but the Cardinals converted him into a reliever because his blazing fastball seemed to lose steam after three or four innings. The results were immediate. By the end of the 1985 season, Worrell was in St. Louis saving games. When the Cardinals won the pennant, he pitched in all four games against the Dodgers. In Game 5 of the World Series, he tied a record by striking out six straight Royals.

In 1986, Worrell overpowered hitters. His 36 saves led the league and set a record for the most ever by a rookie. His 33 saves in 1987 and another 32 the next year made him the first player in major league history to notch 30 saves in each of his first three seasons. But late in 1989, Worrell developed elbow trouble and missed the next two seasons recovering from arm and shoulder surgery.

The Cardinals signed veteran Lee Smith to replace him, and when Worrell returned in 1992, it was as Smith's set-up man. But Worrell wanted to be a closer and so signed with the Los Angeles Dodgers as a free agent in 1993. There, he spent the next five years in the bullpen. Beginning in 1995, he had three straight years with at least 30 saves and his 44 saves in 1996 led the league. He retired after the 1997 season at age 37. His 129 saves as a Cardinal rank second on the team's all-time list.

Joe Magrane
Pitcher, 1987 - 1990; 1992 - 1993

Joe Magrane was a big, strong left-hander whose career was cut short by injuries. A first-round draft pick of the Cardinals, Magrane was a University of Arizona All-American who breezed through the minor leagues on the strength of his blazing fastball and devastating curveball.

Promoted to the majors early in 1987, Magrane won his first start. His third outing, he threw a shut-out. Despite elbow trouble, he went 9-7 his first year and finished third in the voting for National League Rookie of the Year. In 1988, he pitched brilliantly, but suffered from abysmal run support. The Cardinals scored a total of 13 runs in his nine losses. His 2.18 ERA won him the league's ERA crown despite his 5-9 record, making him the first pitcher with a losing record to win the title. His five victories included three shut-outs, highlighted by a one-hitter at Wrigley Field in August.

In 1989, Magrane was at his best. His 18 victories led the team and made him the winningest left-hander in the league. He threw three shut-outs, nine complete games and put together a string of 22 scoreless innings. But the stress of pitching 234 innings took its toll. Despite notching 18 wins before the end of August, Magrane failed to win any of his last six starts.

1990 was a bad year for Magrane and even worse for the Cardinals. The team played so poorly that manager Whitey Herzog quit in July. Again, Magrane was the victim of poor run support and lost his first six starts before finishing with a 10-17 record. It was also his last healthy season in the majors. The next spring, he underwent elbow surgery and missed almost two full years. When he returned, his effectiveness was gone. He went 9-12 over parts of two seasons before being traded to the California Angels late in 1993. Magrane won six games in the American League before retiring in 1996. He later became a broadcaster for the Tampa Bay Devil Rays.

Tom Pagnozzi
Catcher, 1987 - 1998

Tom Pagnozzi spent parts of 12 seasons behind the plate for the Cardinals and won three Gold Glove awards, but competition and injuries limited him to three seasons as an everyday player.

An eighth-round draft choice, Pagnozzi was considered a good catching prospect because of the strength of his offense. But two broken wrists cost him almost a full season in the minors and in 1987, his promotion to the majors was put on hold when the team traded for veteran catcher Tony Pena. Pagnozzi spent two years as Pena's backup and continued that role after the arrival of rookie catcher Todd Zeile, who became the Cardinals' everyday catcher in 1990. But Zeile was moved to third base late in the season and Pagnozzi finally had a chance to show his stuff.

In 1991, Pagnozzi played exceptional defense, throwing out 47 percent of base stealers and winning his first Gold Glove award. The next year, he was named to the All-Star team and tied a National League record for catchers by committing only one error all season. But knee surgery in 1993 and 1994 cost him considerable time on the disabled list and a home-plate collision cut short his 1995 season. Finally healthy, Pagnozzi returned in 1996 with the best offensive year of his career. He batted .270 with a career-high 13 home runs and 55 RBI.

But Pagnozzi couldn't stay healthy. In 1997, leg injuries limited him to 25 games. Finally, late in the 1998 season, the Cardinals released the 36-year-old. In announcing his retirement, Pagnozzi played down his success, telling reporters, "For me to remain almost 12 years in the same spot was an accomplishment. I was lucky. For a guy who can't run, can't hit and all he can do is throw, that's a good career."

Bob Tewksbury
Pitcher, 1989 - 1994

Veteran Bob Tewksbury spent seven years in the Yankees organization and two with the Cubs before signing with the Cardinals as a minor-league free agent in 1989. In the minors, Tewksbury's arm problems convinced him he needed a new strategy. He studied videotape of the best pitchers and began to develop an uncanny control of his pitches. And he began winning. His 13 wins for Louisville in 1989 got him a second chance in the majors. He won 10 games in 1990 and 11 the next year.

In 1992, he become the ace of the St. Louis staff. His 16-5 record was the best winning percentage in the National League and his 2.16 ERA ranked second. His success was due in large part to not issuing any free passes to hitters. Tewksbury allowed a miniscule 20 walks in 233 innings of work. His ratio of walks for every nine innings pitched was the lowest in the majors in 60 years. In 1993, Tewksbury won a team-high 17 games and added to his growing reputation as the game's stingiest pitcher. At one point, he threw 55 consecutive innings without allowing a base on balls.

But in 1994, he won just 12 games and his ERA ballooned. Tewksbury signed with the Texas Rangers as a free agent for the 1995 season. He spent another three years with the Padres and Twins before retiring after the 1998 season.

Todd Zeile
Catcher and Third baseman, 1989 - 1995

Todd Zeile was supposed to be the Cardinals' answer to Johnny Bench.

His first full season in the minors, Zeile hit 25 home runs and drove in 106 runs. In 1989, USA Today named him the minor-league Player of the Year. In a poll of minor-league managers, he was rated among the best catching prospects in professional ball.

In 1990, the Cardinals tapped Zeile for the everyday catching job and as a hitter, he lived up to his billing. His 15 home runs, the most on the team, were the most by a Cardinals rookie in 35 years. And behind the plate, he threw out a respectable 34 percent of base stealers. So it was a big surprise to everyone when the Cardinals suddenly announced that they were moving Zeile to third base a month before the end of the season.

Learning a new position at the major-league level is never an easy task and Zeile struggled with his fielding. In 1991, he committed 25 errors and led National League third basemen in this dubious category. But at the plate, he was rock solid, batting .280 and leading the team in home runs and RBI. In 1993, while knocking in 103 runs, his 33 errors were the most by any Cardinals player in 30 years.

In 1995, the Cardinals shifted Zeile again, this time to first base. But when they couldn't come to terms over a new contract, St. Louis traded him to the Chicago Cubs six weeks into the season. Starting in 1996, Zeile played for six different teams over the next six seasons.

Bernard Gilkey
Outfielder, 1990 - 1995

Baseball wasn't even Bernard Gilkey's best sport at University City High School in St Louis. He was an all-metro basketball star, but he longed to play the outfield at Busch Stadium like his childhood hero, Lou Brock. It wasn't easy, but after six years in the minors, a strong spring training earned Gilkey the starting left-field job for Opening Day 1991. Gilkey's season was interrupted by a broken thumb and pulled leg muscle, but in 1992, he batted .302 and had a team-high 13-game hitting streak.

The next season, he matured into a terrific all-around player. Among outfielders, he tied for league leader with 19 assists. And at the plate, his confidence improved as his run production increased. He batted .305 and led the club in extra base hits and runs scored. But a sub-par 1994 saw his offensive numbers drop and his playing time reduced.

1995 was Gilkey's last season in St. Louis. On a team that struggled to score runs, the front office wanted more offense from the left-field position. His 17 home runs and 69 RBI got Gilkey traded to the New York Mets at season's end. In New York, Gilkey put together the monster year the Cardinals had hoped for. He hit .317 with 30 home runs and 117 RBI. But 1997 was Gilkey's last year as an everyday player. He spent the next six seasons with four different teams, all as a reserve.

Lee Smith
Pitcher, 1990 - 1993

When the Cardinals' bullpen ace, Todd Worrell, was lost for the season in 1990, the club went looking for an established closer. Their search landed one of the game's all-time greats.

Lee Smith spent the previous 10 seasons with the Cubs and the Red Sox and was the game's most intimidating figure on the mound. There was never any guessing with Smith. Everyone in the park knew what was coming. The trick was being able to hit his exploding fastball. Smith's three years in St. Louis were among the best of his long and distinguished career.

In 1991, Smith set a team record and led the National League with 47 saves. He was almost automatic, saving 89 percent of the leads he inherited. The next year, his 43 saves again led the league. He also demonstrated his stamina by appearing in 70 games, becoming the only pitcher in major league history to have 11 straight seasons with at least 60 appearances. In 1994, Smith again notched 43 saves and made his third straight All-Star team. But with the Cardinals in third place late in the season, he was dealt to the Yankees for prospects.

Smith had two big seasons left as he began shifting teams almost every year. His 33 saves for Baltimore in 1994 led all American League relievers, and in 1995, he saved 37 games for the California Angels. Smith retired with 478 career saves after the 1997 season.

Ray Lankford
Outfielder, 1990 - 2001

Ray Lankford's power and speed combined to make him one of the Cardinals' best offensive players for more than a decade. A gifted all-around athlete, Lankford spent four years in the minors before joining in the Cardinals late in 1990. In the majors, he put his speed to good use, leading the league with 15 triples as a rookie and stealing more than 40 bases in each of his first two years. But at the plate, he was prone to strike-outs. In 1992, he hit .293 with 20 home runs and 86 RBI, but he led the league with 147 strike-outs.

In 1995, Lankford became the first Cardinals player since Stan Musial in 1948 to lead the team in home runs and stolen bases in the same season. As he matured, Lankford grew into a leader on and off the field. His defensive play in centerfield remained strong, with only one error in 1996. When the Cardinals won a division title that year, Lankford was the offensive catalyst, stealing 35 bases and scoring 100 runs.

Lankford blossomed into one of the game's best all-around players in 1997. He returned from off-season shoulder surgery to make his first All-Star team by hitting 31 home runs and driving in 98 runs, while batting .295. The next year was even better. Although he struck out 151 times, Lankford punished opposing pitchers with 37 doubles, 31 home runs and 105 RBI.

But off-season knee surgery in 1999 slowed Lankford on the bases and at the plate. As he played less, his batting average dropped and his power numbers fell. Looking to add pitching for the stretch run in 2001, the Cardinals traded Lankford to San Diego for starter Woody Williams.

Joe Torre
Manager, 1990 - 1995

Joe Torre's five years as manager of the Cardinals produced three winning seasons, but no division titles. Torre took over when Whitey Herzog resigned suddenly in August 1990. Previously, he had managed the New York Mets for five years and the Atlanta Braves for three, winning a division title in 1982 and finishing second twice.

With St. Louis, Torre inherited a team that had failed to meet expectations. Herzog's three World Series appearances in the 1980s had spoiled Cardinals fans. But the St. Louis franchise in the early 90s seemed to be in a state of flux. Player turnover was high, and the mix needed to win a championship never came together. Injuries among pitchers undermined the 1991 and 1992 seasons and when the club hit 118 home runs in 1993, the most in 30 years, the club played shoddy defense and had only one starter with more than 11 wins. In the strike-shortened season of 1994, the pitching staff had a 5.14 ERA, the worst by Cardinals pitchers in more than 100 years.

When the team stumbled badly out of the gate in 1995, Torre paid the price. He was fired on June 16. He resurfaced the next season in New York, this time with the Yankees. Beginning in 1996, Torre led the Bronx bombers to four World Series titles in his first six seasons.

Ozzie Smith
Busch Stadium, 1995

Not since the days of Stan Musial had one player so captured the hearts and minds of Cardinals fans. Throughout his 15 years in St. Louis, shortstop Ozzie Smith was the city's most beloved sports icon. Although his last season as an everyday player came in 1993, fans still flocked to the ballpark hoping to see "The Wizard's" glove work and be spellbound one more time.

Smith accommodated his many fans and spearheaded numerous civic and charitable causes. In 1988, he opened a restaurant and published his autobiography. In 1992, he was named St. Louis Man of the Year. Smith personified style and class and his fans loved him for it.

Brian Jordan
Outfielder, 1992 - 1998

Like his Atlanta Falcons teammate Deion Sanders, Brian Jordan was a two-sport professional athlete. Jordan spent three seasons as a Falcons defensive back before giving up football to concentrate on baseball, but injuries from the gridiron delayed his success on the diamond. It wasn't until 1995, his fourth year with the Cardinals, that Jordan was healthy enough to play every day. And play he did. He led the team in hits and stolen bases, while slugging 22 home runs and driving in 81 runs.

In 1996, Jordan hit .310 and drove in 104 runs to lead the Cardinals to the playoffs. There, his 10 postseason hits led the team and included two game-winning home runs. His ninth-inning shot against San Diego won Game 3 and completed a St. Louis sweep. In the National League Championship Series against the Braves, Jordan's eighth-inning home run won Game 4 to put the Cardinals up three games to one before Atlanta roared back to take the series

in seven games.

Jordan's football mentality carried over to baseball, where his aggressive style often left him limping. He also developed a reputation as one of the game's best clutch hitters. In 1996, his .422 average with runners in scoring position led the National League. But wrist and back injuries cost him all but two months of the 1997 season. A rigorous off-season conditioning program helped Jordan rebound with a big season in 1998. He hit .316 with 25 homers and 91 RBI. His big bat also provided protection to teammate Mark McGwire as he chased, and eventually broke, Roger Maris' single-season home-run record.

But Jordan was a free agent after the 1998 season and was allowed to sign with the Braves. With Atlanta, he drove in a career-high 115 runs in 1999 before being traded to the Los Angeles Dodgers for the 2002 season.

Donovan Osborne
Pitcher, 1992 - 1993; 1995 - 1999

Lefty Donovan Osborne was a first-round draft pick who couldn't stay healthy. He was called up from the minors in 1992 and made an immediate impact. In his first five starts, he chalked up three wins and an ERA of 1.23. In May, he retired 24 straight Padres, but got a no-decision when the bullpen couldn't hold a 1-0 lead with two outs in the ninth. By season's end, he had won 11 games. In 1993, he had the lowest ERA among Cardinals starters, but suffered several tough losses and was 10-7 before shoulder problems sidelined him for the final month of the season.

Osborne sat out the 1994 season recovering from shoulder surgery and the first half of 1995 with elbow problems. When he returned, he was wildly inconsistent, leading the team in strike-outs and home runs allowed. During spring training in 1996, Osborne suffered broken ribs in an automobile accident. That season, he won 13 games and again led the team in ERA. In the playoffs, he won Game 3 of the National League Championship Series by beating the Braves, 3-2.

But every time Osborne appeared ready to become the ace of the staff, injuries put him on the shelf. He missed four months in 1997 because of hernia and groin problems and ended the season, 3-7. The Cardinals front office grew weary of waiting for Osborne and released him after the 1999 season. He spent the next two years out of baseball, trying to get healthy. Finally, in 2002, he joined the Chicago Cubs' bullpen as a reliever.

Dennis Eckersley
Pitcher, 1996 - 1997

One of manager Tony LaRussa's first moves in St. Louis was to locate a reliable closer. He chose Dennis Eckersley, someone he knew from his days managing in Oakland. Eckersley had pocketed 320 saves during his nine years with the A's, twice leading the American League.

With St. Louis, Eckersley was money in the bank. He saved 30 of 34 games in 1996. His pinpoint control allowed him to walk just six hitters in 60 innings of work. He was perfect in the postseason, closing out all three wins against the San Diego Padres. And in the NLCS against the Atlanta Braves, he had a save in Game 3 and a victory in Game 4.

The next season, "the Eck" struggled with control and blew seven save opportunities, even though he rang up 36 saves. A free agent, he opted to sign with the Boston Red Sox for the 1998 season so that he could be at home with his wife and kids. He retired at age 43 after one final season in Boston.

Tony LaRussa
Manager, 1996 -

Manager Tony LaRussa brought stability and a winning attitude to the Cardinals. Hired to replace Joe Torre after the 1995 season, LaRussa was a veteran of 17 American League seasons, having won a division title with the Chicago White Sox and taken the Oakland A's to three straight World Series appearances.

His first year in St. Louis, LaRussa and the Cardinals won 87 games and the National League Central Division title. The Cardinals took a three-game lead in the championship series against the Atlanta Braves, but couldn't find a way to win and return to the World Series. 1997 was a disaster as the team lost 89

games while using a record 51 players, including 24 pitchers. And while 1998 was highlighted by Mark McGwire's historic home-run chase, the Cardinals played .500 ball and finished third in the NL Central. But the team's new owners agreed to increase the payroll and in 2000, the Cardinals returned to the postseason. They won 95 games, their highest total since 1987. They also got revenge on Atlanta by sweeping them in the division series before falling to the New York Mets in the NLCS. The next year, LaRussa led the Cardinals back to the playoffs as the NL wild-card team.

Ozzie Smith
Busch Stadium, 1996

After 19 major league seasons, 41-year-old Ozzie Smith decided to hang up his glove. On September 28, 1996, the Cardinals retired his uniform number in a pre-game ceremony as family, fans and teammates looked on. Smith's 2,511 games at shortstop rank second on baseball's all-time list, just behind Hall of Famer Luis Aparicio. Smith was selected to 15 All-Star games and his 13 Gold Gloves are the most ever by a National League player. Smith's 433 career stolen bases are the third most by a Cardinal. In 2002, Smith was elected to the Hall of Fame on the first ballot.

Andy Benes
Pitcher, 1996 - 1997; 2000 -

George Kissell
Instructor, 1946 -

Andy Benes' best season of his long major-league career was his first in St. Louis. Signed as a free agent in 1996, Benes was a big, strong power pitcher who had been a consistent winner his six previous seasons, most with San Diego.

With St. Louis, Benes got off to a rocky start, but ended the season with 18 wins, second most in the National League. He was at his best down the stretch. As the Cardinals surged towards the playoffs, Benes was the anchor of the starting rotation, going 17-3 over the final four months of the season. He won his only start in the division playoffs against his old team, the Padres. In Game 1 of the National League Championship Series, Benes squared off against Atlanta's John Smoltz and left after six innings with the game tied, 2-2, before the Braves rallied to win, 4-2.

But Benes got a late start in 1997 because of a pulled rib cage muscle and with his record at 10-7, his season ended when a pitch broke a finger on his pitching hand while batting against the Rockies. Benes joined Arizona for the next two years, going 27-25 before re-signing with St. Louis in 2000. He went 12-9 his first year back, and had the dubious distinction of giving up four home runs in the first inning of a game at Houston. In the postseason, Benes secured the Cardinals' only victory in the NLCS against the New York Mets.

But injuries in 2002 cost him the first half of the season.

For nearly 50 years, George Kissell has taught young players the Cardinals' way of playing ball. Since 1946, he has managed, coached and scouted in the Cardinals' minor-league system. From 1969 to 1975, he was a major league coach in St. Louis. His ability to teach the game's fundamentals has ensured that the club's top prospects were properly prepared for the big leagues. In 1999, the Cardinals honored Kissell with a plaque at Busch Stadium for his many years of service.

J.D. Drew
Outfielder, 1998 -

J.D. Drew made headlines before he played a single major league game. Drafted second in 1997, he refused to sign with the Philadelphia Phillies because the club wouldn't meet his terms. Instead, he played for the independent St. Paul Saints and then returned for his junior year at Florida State, where he was a consensus All-American and recipient of the Golden Spikes Award as the nation's best amateur player.

In 1998, St. Louis drafted and signed Drew, who spent two months in the minors before joining the Cardinals for the last three weeks of the season. Immediately, Drew showed what the fuss was all about. In his first 14 games, he hit five home runs and drove in 13 runs. But as so often happens, the league's pitchers found his weaknesses and Drew was forced to make some adjustments the next year. He missed six weeks with a leg injury, but ended his first full season in the big leagues with a .242 average, 13 home runs and 19 stolen bases.

2000 was big step forward for Drew. Although he suffered from frequent strike-outs, he ended the year with a .295 average and 18 home runs. His defense also improved as word of his strong arm quickly spread among base runners. In 2001, he grew more patient at the plate, stopped swinging at so many bad pitches and saw a surge in his offensive numbers. Although injuries limited him to 109 games, he batted .323 with 27 home runs and 73 RBI.

Mark McGwire
First baseman, 1997 - 2001

Mark McGwire's arrival in St. Louis midway through the 1997 season was a pivotal event for a franchise that had never had a slugger of his caliber. Of his first 44 hits in a Cardinals uniform, 24 were home runs. Soon, fans began arriving early just to watch his tape-measure home runs during batting practice.

When McGwire surprised everyone by signing a three-year contract extension in September, an instant love affair ignited between the city and "Big Mac." McGwire finished the 1997 season with a career-high 58 home runs. No one could have predicted his encore.

Mark McGwire
September 8, 1998

When Mark McGwire got off to a blazing start in 1998, people wondered whether he might approach Roger Maris' hallowed home-run record. On Opening Day, McGwire hit a grand slam, the first Cardinal ever to do so. He hit a home run in each of the next three games and by the end of April, he had 11. He hit 16 in May and 10 in June, giving him 37 by July 1, a new major league record.

When the Cubs' Sammy Sosa suddenly got hot, McGwire had company in the hunt for a new home-run record. When Sosa hit his 48th on August 19, McGwire hit two to reach 49. Just as in 1961, the nation became captivated by two sluggers sprinting toward the record. McGwire's four home runs in two games against Florida gave him the lead with 59 on September 2. With 21 games left in the season, the only question was when, not if, he would break Maris' mark of 61, a record that had stood for 37 years.

The answer came six days later at Busch Stadium. On Tuesday, September 8, facing the Cubs' Steve Trachsel, McGwire drove a pitch down the left-field line and over the wall. As the stadium erupted, McGwire almost forgot to touch first base. When he finally crossed home plate, he was met by his teammates, his young son, Matt, and Sosa, who came in from right-field to wrap McGwire in a historic bear hug.

Looking on from a box near the Cardinals' dugout were Roger Maris' children. McGwire honored their father by pointing to the sky and exchanging hugs with the Maris family. The game was stopped for a ceremony at home plate. The ball, retrieved by a grounds-crew member, was presented to McGwire as his parents looked on.

With more than two weeks left in the season, the only remaining question was what number would mark the end of McGwire's historic trek.

Matt Morris
Pitcher, 1997 -

Matt Morris has slowly emerged as the ace of the Cardinals' rotation. A first-round pick out of Seton Hall, Morris spent only two years in the minor leagues before joining the Cardinals in 1997. His first year, he went 12-9 and led all National League rookie pitchers in ERA, wins and strike-outs. But a shoulder injury cost him the first half of 1998 and limited him to a 7-5 mark. And during spring training in 1999, he injured his elbow and required reconstructive surgery. He was lost for the entire season while recovering from "Tommy John" surgery.

The Cardinals decided to bring Morris back slowly the next year. He worked exclusively out of the bullpen, never throwing more than three innings at a time. The cautious approach paid big dividends in 2001, when Morris became the workhorse of the staff. He went 22-8, made the All-Star team and developed into the Cardinals' most dependable starter. His 22 wins were the most by a Cardinals pitcher since Bob Gibson's 23 in 1970. His efforts in the postseason were even better. In the division series against Arizona, Morris squared off against Diamondbacks ace Curt Shilling in Games 1 and 5. Morris allowed just two runs in 15 innings of work, but the Cardinals lost both games by a single run.

In 2002, Morris picked up where he left off. He went 10-4 in his first 16 starts to help put the Cardinals in first place at the All-Star break.

Mark McGwire
September 27, 1998

On the last day of the 1998 season, Mark McGwire put an exclamation point on his historic home-run record. Against the Montreal Expos at Busch Stadium, he came to the plate in the third inning and hit number 69. After a walk in the fifth, he took his final at-bat of the season in the seventh inning and hit number 70, closing a storybook season in dramatic fashion. At a post-game press conference, he seemed relieved to have put it behind him.

In 1999, McGwire continued his assault on the record books by hitting another 65 home runs to lead the majors for the fourth straight season. He also led the National League with 147 RBI, the second highest total in franchise history. He hit his 500th career home run on July 5, and by season's end, he had hit a staggering 405 home runs during the 1990s. He thus joined Hall of Famers Babe Ruth and Jimmie Foxx as only the third player to hit 400 home runs in a single decade.

McGwire's 2001 season was marred by back spasms and a bad right knee. He played only 70 games and missed most of the season's second half. He came to the plate mostly as a pinch-hitter, but managed to slug 29 home runs, giving him 583 for his career. When the season ended, he surprised everyone by announcing his retirement at age 38, walking away from the two years and $30 million remaining on his contract.

Rick Ankiel
Pitcher, 1999 -

Rick Ankiel's roller-coaster ride in the majors reached the record books before dipping to the low minor leagues because of control problems.

Ankiel joined the Cardinals' starting rotation in 2000 and had a terrific first year, going 11-7. He struck out 194 batters in 175 innings and broke Dizzy Dean's rookie record of 191 set in 1930. But in the playoffs, things unraveled.

In Game 1 of the division series against Atlanta, with the Cardinals ahead after two innings, 6-0, Ankiel fell apart. Against the next eight batters, he gave up four runs, threw five wild pitches and was pulled from the game. It happened again in Game 2 of the NLCS against the Mets. Ankiel failed to make it out of the first inning, walking three and uncorking two wild pitches.

Ankiel's sudden inability to throw the ball over the plate baffled players and fans alike. When the 2001 season began, he beat Randy Johnson and the Arizona Diamondbacks. But it wasn't long before his throwing problems returned and the Cardinals sent him to the minors. He was demoted to the Appalachian League, the lowest level of the minor leagues. There, he got himself turned around, leading the league in ERA and strike-outs. But in 2002, elbow problems kept him on the shelf for the first half of the season, casting his future in doubt.

Will Clark
First baseman, 2000

Will Clark's brief stay in St. Louis helped power the Cardinals to the 2000 postseason. He took over when first baseman Mark McGwire went down in July and more than filled the bill. In his final 51 games, he batted .345, with 12 home runs and 42 RBI. His clutch hitting and veteran leadership helped propel St. Louis to 95 wins and the NL Central Division crown.

In the playoffs, Clark's bat continued to roar. His first-inning three-run homer in Game 2 of the division series powered the Cardinals to a series sweep over the Atlanta Braves. But his .345 average and 10 hits in the playoffs weren't enough as St. Louis fell to the New York Mets in five games in the NLCS. When the season ended, Clark retired at age 36, saying he wanted to go out on top.

Edgar Renteria
Shortstop, 1999 -

Edgar Renteria's skills in the field and at the plate make him one of the Cardinals' most valuable assets.

Arriving in 1999 from the Florida Marlins, where he'd won a World Series ring two years earlier, Renteria filled the gap left by the retirement of Ozzie Smith. He wasn't as flashy in the field, but he was a bigger offensive threat. In 1999, he led the team in hits, doubles and stolen bases.

The next year, Renteria's 36 doubles led the team and his 76 RBI were the second highest ever by a Cardinals shortstop. His 26 stolen bases also were tops on the club and his 16 home runs were the most ever by a Cardinals shortstop. Renteria made his second All-Star team and was presented a Silver Slugger award as the league's top-hitting shortstop. In the playoffs, he scored five runs in the division series against Atlanta and he had the team's only three stolen bases of the NLCS against the Mets.

In 2001, Renteria got off to a slow start at the plate before catching fire in the last two months of the season. Yet, despite hitting safely in 42 of his final 58 games, his batting average was a career-low .260. He did, however, lead the team in stolen bases for the third straight year and play stellar defense.

Fernando Vina
Second baseman, 2000 -

As the Cardinals' lead-off hitter, Fernando Vina ignites the St. Louis offense. He has a keen eye at the plate and is dedicated to getting on base, no matter the cost. His first season in St. Louis, he was plunked by a pitch 28 times, more than any other batter in the National League and the most by a Cardinals' player in 90 years.
He also led the club with 10 bunt singles and 17 infield hits his first year in St. Louis. In the field, he led the league's second basemen in fielding percentage for two consecutive years, winning his first Gold Glove award in 2001.

In the 2000 playoffs, Vina had a hit in all eight postseason games. His lead-off home run in Game 3 of the division series against Atlanta helped the Cardinals complete the sweep. In 2001, he batted over .300 for the second straight year and was the league's second-toughest hitter to strike out. He hit nine home runs and 56 RBI, both career highs, and his 191 hits were second on the team to Albert Pujols' 194. And when St. Louis faced Arizona in the first round of the playoffs, Vina's .316 average led the team.

It is a mark of his dedication to getting on base that Vina's eight-plus years in the majors include more walks than strike-outs.

Jim Edmonds
Outfielder, 2000 -

A change of scenery recharged Jim Edmond's career and gave the Cardinals one of the most talented all-around players in franchise history.

During his six seasons with the Anaheim Angels, Edmonds made the highlight reels almost nightly because of his sensational outfield play. But his aggressive, all-out style left him playing injured for long stretches of time. And in 1999, with his season marred by injuries and the Angels continuing to lose, the two decided to part company.

In St. Louis, Edmonds' spectacular defensive skills and run production made him an instant fan favorite. In 2000, his 42 home runs, 108 RBI and 103 walks led the team. He became the first Cardinals outfielder to hit more than 40 home runs in one season.

Because of his success, he was named to his second All-Star team. Edmonds was so excited about being in St. Louis that he signed a six-year contract extension after only five weeks with the team. When the Cardinals won the Central Division title and faced the Braves in the playoffs, Edmonds led St. Louis to a three-game sweep. He went eight for 14, with two home runs and seven RBI.

Edmonds' 2001 season was equally productive. He hit .304 with 30 home runs and 110 RBI. In the field, he made only six errors and won his fourth Gold Glove award. He continues to be a cornerstone of the St. Louis offense and his acrobatic play in centerfield ranks him among the game's best glove men.

Mike Matheny
Catcher, 2000 -

Mike Matheny's strong arm and ability to gun down base stealers make him one of the game's best defensive catchers.

His first year in St. Louis, Matheny won a Gold Glove award and led the majors by snaring 51 percent of would-be base stealers. His ability to corral the opposition's running game made up for his lack of hitting. His offense picked up late in the season, when he drove in 19 runs over his last 24 games. But a freak accident with a hunting knife meant he needed surgery and kept him from the playoffs.

In 2001, Matheny's defense remained strong. He threw out 45 percent of base stealers and picked off five base runners, but his batting average plummeted. When his offense didn't pick up in 2002, he began to share time behind the plate.

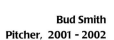

Bud Smith
Pitcher, 2001 - 2002

Bud Smith made history his first season in the majors. On September 3, 2001, he became only the third Cardinals rookie pitcher to throw a no-hitter. Facing the Padres in San Diego, Smith walked four and struck out seven in blanking the Padres, 4-0. It was the highlight of a season that saw him go 6-3 in less than a half season of work. In the playoffs against the Diamondbacks, Smith threw five innings in Game 4, allowing just one run on four hits as the Cardinals evened the series at two wins apiece.

But Smith struggled early in 2002, going 0-5 in his first six starts. He was later traded to the Phillies in the deal for Scott Rolen.

Darryl Kile
Pitcher, 2000 - 2002

Darryl Kile's 20-win season for St. Louis and his no-hitter for Houston will long be overshadowed by his tragic death at age 33.

His third season in St. Louis, Kile became the workhorse of the starting staff, never missing a start and leading the rotation in innings pitched for two straight years. His 20-9 record in 2000 made him the first 20-game winner for the Cardinals in 15 years and along the way, won him a spot on his third All-Star team.

Despite an ERA of 3.09, fifth best in the National League, Kile went 16-11 in 2001. But his record was more the result of poor run support as the Cardinals scored just 20 runs in his 11 losses. The highlight of Kile's season was blanking the Braves for eight innings in a duel against Atlanta ace Greg Maddux on August 1. The Cardinals won, 4-0.

Returning from off-season shoulder surgery, Kile went 5-4 early in the 2002 season. His best performance came on Tuesday, June 17, against the Anaheim Angels at Busch Stadium. Kile pitched into the eighth inning, allowing the Angels one run on six hits on the night that legendary broadcaster Jack Buck died after a long illness at age 77. It was the last game Darryl Kile would ever pitch.

Four days later, Kile was found dead in his Chicago hotel room from what an autopsy would show was severe blockage in the coronary arteries. His death stunned the baseball world. It seemed unimaginable that a professional athlete could simply go to bed and never wake up. The fans and the franchise were rocked by his passing. In a city widely regarded as the best baseball town in the majors, the game suddenly seemed unimportant.

Albert Pujols
Infielder, Outfielder; 2001 -

In 2001, Albert Pujols had one of the greatest debut seasons in franchise history, rewriting the rookie record books with his rare ability to hit for average and power.

Pujols wasn't even in the Cardinals' plans for 2001. After all, he'd spent just one season in the minors, most of it in Class A ball. But a strong spring training and an injury to veteran Bobby Bonilla landed Pujols a slot on the roster and he made the most of it. By the end of April, he was hitting .370 and leading the club in home runs and RBI. His eight long balls in April tied the rookie major league record.

In June, he hit home runs in four straight games. In July, he ran up a 17-game hitting streak, the team's longest of the season. His 37 home runs, 130 RBI, .329 average and 112 runs scored were all tops on the team and made him the first National League rookie ever to reach these four plateaus.

He also became the first Cardinal since Ted Simmons in 1973 to win the club's triple crown, tops in home runs, RBI and batting average — and he did it all while splitting time between four different positions. For his efforts, Pujols was the unanimous choice for the NL Rookie of the Year award and finished fourth in the league's MVP balloting. He also won the Silver Slugger award as the league's top-hitting third baseman.

In 2002, Pujols got off to another strong start. His talents will have a lot to do with how far the Cardinals go towards winning another championship.

Photograph Index

Photograph Credits

Cincinnati Enquirer, The:
58

Goldstein, Dennis:
frontispiece, 11, 17, 21(right), 38(left), 39, 46(left), 48(left), 71, 104, 111(left), 113

Knight, Bill:
150, 154, 156, 157, 160, 165, 170, 182, 183, 190, 196, 207

Knoll, Dan:
51

Loughman, Bill:
33, 38(right), 42(right), 49, 56, 61, 63, 64, 69, 73, 80, 105, 122(right), 133, 139, 143

McWilliams, Doug:
140, 144(right), 145, 146, 148, 149, 152, 153

Mumby, Mike:
10, 12, 26, 31, 42(left), 60, 92

National Baseball Hall of Fame Library:
Cooperstown, N.Y.
8, 9, 16, 18, 23, 24(left), 25, 28, 30, 32(left), 35, 36, 41, 43, 45, 54, 55, 66, 68, 70, 72, 74(left), 75, 77, 81, 82, 83, 86, 87, 88, 89, 90, 91, 94, 96, 98, 99, 109, 110, 112(left), 114, 118, 119, 122(left), 125, 126(right), 142, 144(left), 158, 166, 172

SABR/Ottoson files:
24(right), 32(right)

Stang, Mark:
13, 78, 95, 159(right), 161, 178(left)

St. Louis Mercantile Library at
The University of Missouri-St. Louis:
14, 19, 21(left), 22, 27, 29, 34, 37, 40, 46(right), 47, 48(right), 50, 52, 57, 62, 74(right), 76, 84, 85, 97, 100, 101, 102, 103, 108, 111(right), 112(right), 117, 121, 123, 124, 126(left), 128, 132, 135, 136, 138, 141, 147, 155, 159(left), 162, 163, 167, 168, 171, 173, 174, 177, 178(right)

St. Louis Post-Dispatch:
137, 151, 164, 169, 179, 180, 181, 184, 185, 186, 187, 188, 189, 191(right), 195, 197, 201(right)

The Sporting News:
15, 20, 44, 59, 65, 67, 93, 106, 107, 120, 127, 129, 130, 131, 134, 175, 176, 192, 193, 194

Transcendental Graphics:
53, 79, 115, 116

Trombetti, Skip:
191(left), 198, 199, 200, 201(left), 202, 203

**Gussie Busch and Whitey Herzog
World Series, 1982**

After the Cardinals' come-from-behind victory over the Milwaukee Brewers in Game 7 of the 1982 World Series, manager Whitey Herzog presented owner Gussie Busch with the championship trophy. Little did Cardinals fans realize that 20 years later, they would still be waiting for another World Series title.

To order additional copies of *Cardinals Collection*, or for information about other titles currently available from Orange Frazer Press, please call **1–800–852–9332**, or visit our website at **orangefrazer.com**. Address inquiries to:
Orange Frazer Press
P.O. Box 214
37½ West Main Street
Wilmington, OH 45177.